D-DAY JAPAN

JAPAN

*The Truth About
the Invasion of Japan,
its War Crimes, and
the Atomic Bomb*

GENERAL RAYMOND DAVIS
MEDAL OF HONOR
AND JUDGE DAN WINN

Acclaim Press
MORLEY, MISSOURI

Acclaim Press
— *Your Next Great Book* —
P.O. Box 238
Morley, MO 63767
(573) 472-9800
www.acclaimpress.com

Designer: M. Frene Melton
Cover Design: M. Frene Melton

Library of Congress Cataloging-in-Publication Data

Winn, Dan.
  D-day Japan / by Dan Winn and Raymond Davis.
    p. cm.
  Includes bibliographical references.
  ISBN-13: 978-1-935001-16-4 (alk. paper)
  ISBN-10: 1-935001-16-7
  1. World War, 1939-1945--Japan--Historiography. 2. World War,
1939-1945--Historiography. I. Davis, Raymond, 1915-2003. II. Title.

  D743.42W56 2009
  940.54'0952--dc22

                                        2009000939

First Printing: 2009
Printed in the United States of America
10 9 8 7 6 5 4 3 2 1

Contents

Dedication

This book is dedicated to my wife, Knox Davis.

—Ray Davis

This book is dedicated from me to my deceased mother and father, Mary Peace Winn and Frank M. Winn; and to my deceased sister, Lt. Jean Winn, who served in the Navy WAVES during World War II. I believe she was the first officer candidate recruit from the state of Georgia.

—Dan Winn

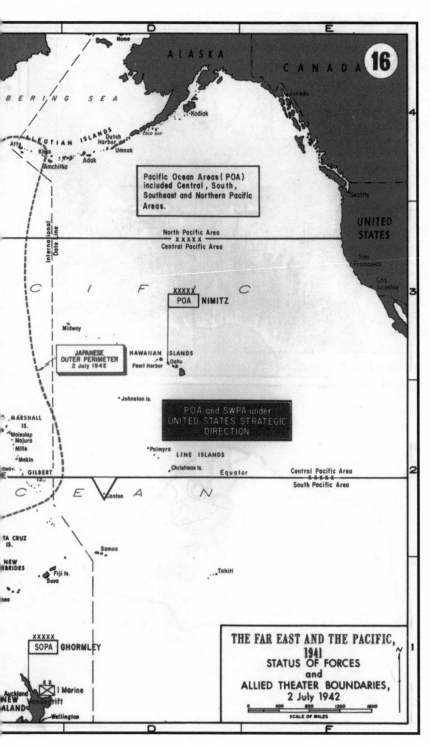

D · **E**

16

ALASKA

CANADA

Nome

Juneau

BERING SEA

· Kodiak

ALEUTIAN ISLANDS

Dutch
Harbor

COLD BAY

Attu

Kiska

Umnak

Adak

Amchitka

Seattle

UNITED
STATES

International Date Line

North Pacific Area
XXXXX
Central Pacific Area

San
Francisco

Los
Angeles

P A C I F I C

Pacific Ocean Areas (POA)
included Central, South,
Southeast and Northern Pacific
Areas.

XXXXX
POA NIMITZ

Midway

JAPANESE
OUTER PERIMETER
2 July 1942

HAWAIIAN ISLANDS
Pearl Harbor   Oahu

· Johnston Is.

POA and SWPA under
UNITED STATES STRATEGIC
DIRECTION

MARSHALL
IS.
· Maleolap
· Majuro
· Mili
· Makin

· Palmyra

LINE ISLANDS

· Christmas Is.

GILBERT
IS.

Equator

Central Pacific Area
XXXXX
South Pacific Area

O C E A N

· Canton

TA CRUZ
IS.

Samoa

NEW
HEBRIDES

Fiji Is.
Suva

· Tahiti

XXXXX
SOPA GHORMLEY

Auckland
Vandegrift
NEW
ZEALAND

XX
I Marine

Wellington

**THE FAR EAST AND THE PACIFIC,
1941
STATUS OF FORCES
and
ALLIED THEATER BOUNDARIES,
2 July 1942**

0   400   800   1200   1600

SCALE OF MILES

D · **E**

— 11 —

Brigadier General Paul W. Tibbets, pilot of the Enola Gay *that dropped the atomic bomb on Hiroshima in 1945.*

The crew of the Enola Gay *before takeoff for Hiroshima. L-R, standing: Lt. Col. John Porter, Capt. Theodore J. Van Kirk, Maj. Thomas W. Ferebee, Col. Paul W. Tibbets, Capt. Robert A. Lewis, and Lt. Jacob Beser. Kneeling: Sgt. Joseph Stiborik, SSgt. George R. Caron, Pfc. Richard H. Nelson, Sgt. Robert H. Shumard, and SSgt. Wyatt Duzenbury.*

Foreword

Along with all veterans of World War II, most military personnel, and most informed Americans, I was appalled at the anti-U.S.A., anti-military and anti-Truman display of the *Enola Gay*, proposed by the National Air and Space Museum of the Smithsonian Institution in 1995.

As Judge Dan Winn asked me to join him in presenting this book to the world in the hope that it will give a true historic perspective on the atomic bomb and its proper use by the United States of America, it is an honor to participate in this project.

From my experience on Peleliu, and the evidence we point out in the book, an invasion of Japan could have sacrificed almost the entire Marine Corps force, along with a large portion of our Navy and Army.

—General Raymond Davis (Ret.)
Medal of Honor–U.S. Marine Corps
Assistant Commandant U.S. Marine Corps

Brigadier General Paul W. Tibbets, Jr.

For over fifty years I have been listening to the Japanese and many factually incorrect historians criticize President Harry Truman, the use of the atomic bomb, and me and my crew for dropping the Bomb on Hiroshima. The ongoing, near-total distortion of history, along with the proposed *Enola Gay* Exhibit at the National Air and Space Museum, completed a blatantly incorrect picture favoring the Japanese propaganda campaign regarding the Bomb and the end of the war.

I was delighted when Judge Dan Winn approached me about publishing a book revealing the many atrocities performed by the Japanese and supporting the use of the Bomb to end the horribly barbaric war. This book is intended to counter those revisionists dominating the media and present a true historical account for the present and future generations. What you are about to read will shock you, and it should. It is long overdue that these activities and statistics be revealed and included in our history books. Readers will finally understand why President Truman and our country had no choice but to stop the Japanese as quickly as possible, and that included dropping the Bomb.

I repeat what I said in my book, *Flight of the Enola Gay:*

"On August 6, 1945 as the Enola Gay *approached the Japanese city of Hiroshima, I fervently hoped for success in the first use of a nuclear type weapon. To me it meant putting an end to the fighting and the consequent loss of lives. In fact, I viewed my mission as one to save lives rather than to take them. The intervening year has brought me so many letters and personal contacts with individuals who maintain that they would not be alive today if it had not been for what I did. Likewise, I have been asked in letters and to my face if I was*

not conscience stricken for the loss of life I caused by dropping the first atomic bomb. To those who ask, I quickly reply, 'Not in the Least.' This is still true."

After thirty-five years I still have a clear conscience about the Bomb, as I know President Truman did.

—*Brigadier General Paul W. Tibbets*
Pilot of the *Enola Gay* that dropped the
atomic bomb on Hiroshima in 1945

Introduction

In August of 1945, the United States of America used the atomic bomb to destroy the Japanese cities of Hiroshima and Nagasaki. Japan surrendered, thus ending the tragedy that has come to be known as World War II. The dropping of the Bomb was one of the most important historical occurrences of all time.

The necessity, humanity and wisdom of President Harry Truman's decision to use the Bomb has long been the subject of books, debates, discussions, and commentary on the part of the news media, academia, and citizenry in general. President Truman's position was that the Bomb saved many lives, not only American lives, but lives of those in our Allied forces, lives in China and, yes, even the lives of Japanese civilians. Because so many lives would be spared from the horrific onslaught of a ground invasion, there was no better choice than the Bomb. Veterans of the war and most people from that generation know this to be true. Somehow, that knowledge, in itself, will not prevail historically if we are to give credence to those who constantly distort and destroy what could otherwise be regarded as plain and simple TRUTH.

For over sixty years now, servicemen from that era who prepared for the invasion, have resented the revisionist claim that their millions of lives were expendable. They resent any notion that their lives were less valuable than those of the city of Hiroshima and Nagasaki.

Therefore, this book serves as an answer to these simple questions:

1. Would the Japanese have surrendered without the Bomb?
   Conclusive evidence is that they would not.
2. Did the Bomb save more lives than it took?
   It spared more lives, well into the millions.
3. Should we have doubts about the Bomb being correct?
   We should have no doubts, but live with an absolute clear conscience.

In a secretly intercepted communication among the Japanese high command, Foreign Minister Mamoru Shigemitsu embarked on a campaign of what he referred to as "propaganda" to immediately discredit use of the Bomb. The purpose of this propaganda was to divert attention from Japan's horrendous treatment of prisoners of war as well as their merciless killing rampage through China and Asia, which had been occurring for decades.

For over sixty years, every August 6th, there is a highly publicized visit to Hiroshima by the Japan leadership. The Emperor heads the event, and there is much deploring of the use of the Bomb. The United States is referred to as "barbaric." And though there have been many excellent articles and books which support the use of the Bomb, the historical correctness of that action has been somewhat overshadowed by the incessant depiction of Hiroshima victims and seeming endorsement of the Japanese view that it was not necessary. Tragically, some have made a totally unacceptable comparison of it to the Holocaust.

This anti-American slant on the use of the Bomb has, in fact, been furthered by some of our own anti-bomb theorists. It was disturbing to watch a televised documentary of the war, which was hosted by ABC's Peter Jennings in 1996. It appeared his sympathy was fully aligned with the Japanese. My research has led me to one particular book wherein the authors (Lifton & Mitchell) claimed that the Bomb "has weighed heavily on our national conscience" and that we have a "raw nerve" over Hiroshima. The authors maintained that the Bomb has "eluded reasoned discussion." The natural explanation for this is that nine out of ten programs by a misinformed media have been anti-nuclear in content. There has never been anything resembling a debate format relative to the Bomb.

Even so, the vast majority of Americans approved of the A-Bomb. They accepted the President's statement that it was correct given the treacherous attack on Pearl Harbor, which launched our involvement into World War II. Many have said that America was justified in ending the war with the Bomb. The propaganda continues, though, and this revisionism reached a crescendo during the time of the proposed *Enola Gay* exhibit at the National Air and Space Museum which was to commemorate the end of WWII in the Pacific. The exhibit, in the heart of the Smithsonian Institution at our nation's Capitol, was orchestrated by some wild politically correct professors (headed by Martin Harwit) who lacked real insight into the reasons for the use of the Bomb. They lacked reasonable analysis for its use, but did have an anti-nuclear agenda.

These distasteful and flawed narrations of distorted history have caused many who care about true historical accounting (including myself) to speak out with our views on the subject. This book, in part, serves as a challenge to those like Gar Alperovitz, Peter Kuznick, Kai Bird, Harwit, Jennings, Lifton and Mitchell in the hope that they would participate in a national forum with us and participate in "a reasoned discussion" on both sides of the A-Bomb issue. Beyond this, it should be known that a feeling of resentment has been building up within us veterans…a feeling which would have been best reflected in the original title for this book—"Shut Up About the Damned A-Bomb!"

The facts that follow are true and should be conveyed to all United States citizens and students who pass through their respective institution of higher learning. The use of the atomic bomb should never reflect adversely on the morality or humanity of the United States of America.

—*Judge Dan Winn*

Note:

The original edition of this book was written while I was still active as a Senior Superior Court Judge in Georgia. While my facts and figures were correct, I did not reference or annotate well, and, in my zeal to promote my view and that of all World War II military veterans regarding the atomic bomb, I was most abrasive in criticizing the Revisionists who opposed use of the Bomb.

This edition, I believe, corrects those errors.

Readers did not know the validity of many of my sources. I did not show the basis for some huge figures, not used before, which have raised questions as to their authenticity. For example, 30,000,000 Chinese and Southeast Asians were slaughtered by the Japanese during their aggression in China beginning prior to 1931 and until after the atomic bomb was dropped, August 1945. Casualties to U.S. military personnel, in the planned invasion of the Japan home islands to be in one million to two million range. Also noteworthy (but seldom mentioned in historical accounts of the planned invasion), this book's statement that the military and civilian casualties to the Japanese could be 20,000,000.

In the text I will show you by credible authors, indisputable figures and logical conclusions that all these figures were properly used, then and now.

In the Bibliography sections are listed those authors whom I consider as credible historians, and I've also listed those who I believe have distorted history because of their agenda. The revisionists all use specific indefensible figures as the basis for their conclusion as to the number of U.S. casualties to be expected in the planned invasion of Japan, to begin November 1, 1945, viz.: 20,000 to 46,000 (maximum). In the main text it will show that these figures, if ever having any valid basis, were for many months before the atomic bomb was used, and did not, could not, take into account the rapid influx of Japanese divisions into Kyushu, escalating their troop strength from 100,000 in early 1944 to about 228,000 on April 28, 1945, then to almost 600,000 by Aug. 2, 1945 and with actually 900,000 assigned by the Japanese for the defense of Kyushu (Central Intelligence Agency—*Signals Intelligence*, see pages 3 and 46).

When the learned Professors were insisting on using 20,000 to 46,000 as the casualty estimates to U.S. forces in the coming invasion of the Japanese islands of Kyushu and Honshu, someone commented that, "A Baboon with a Ouija board could come up with better figures!"

Those indefensibly low figures, by the revisionist authors, will be readily apparent to any reader looking at the maps of Kyushu, the number of U.S. troops invading and the increased Japanese troop strength there; add that to the terrible invasion conditions of Kamikaze planes, women and children as suicide bombers, and underground defenses patterned after those on Iwo Jima, explained in the main text.

Gar Alperovitz, maybe the most vocal and persistent of the anti-Bomb activists, in his book, *Atomic Diplomacy* 1st Ed. 1965, 2nd Ed. 1985 and then 30 years later, in *Hiroshima, The Decision to Use the Atomic Bomb*, persisted in calling the proposed Kyushu landings, (with over 600,000 defending Japanese troops, opposing 766,700 invading U.S. forces) an INITIAL PRELIMINARY LANDING. This D-Day (Japan) would involve five times the number of forces involved in the D-Day landing in Normandy, in Europe, which was 150,000 Allied troops.

I detail the exact quotes from Alperovitz' books later in the text. This writing is typical of the authors I tell you have 'no credibility', as they show no understanding of the war against the Japanese, or of war in general. They demonstrate only a clear bias against the military, the U.S. and the atomic bomb.

Preface

The *Enola Gay* Crew
(509th Composite Bomb Group Reunion)
July 31, 1997

There have been some intimations or rumors concerning the *Enola Gay* crew and particularly concerning their mental health as it related to memories of the dropping of the atomic bomb.

This author had the distinct privilege of attending a reunion of the 509th Composite Bomb Group in Dayton, Ohio on July 31, 1997. I had occasion, at length and very closely, to associate with members of Brig. General Paul W. Tibbets, Jr.'s crew; Viz. Dutch Van Kirk, navigator; Tom Ferebee, bombardier; and Richard Nelson, radio operator.

This writer can say, without equivocation, that none of these members of the crew had the slightest indication of any negative residual feelings of any kind from the mission to drop the Bomb.

They were as mentally alert as anyone could imagine, and Brig. General Paul W. Tibbets, Jr. was as sharp as anyone could imagine although he was eighty-four years of age.

One could know, in listening and talking to all of them, that they had the positive feeling of regret that the atomic bomb was necessary, but they have absolutely no regret that the Bomb had been used.

In speaking with General Tibbets, this author felt that he could not begin to entertain any feelings of remorse for dropping the Bomb because, before even thinking of that, he would think of the many Marines and many Army personnel who would be killed and maimed in an invasion of the homeland islands, and also the many Navy personnel and ships that would have suffered tremendous casualties both to the landing troops and the Navy.

Chronology

JAPAN — SUPER HOLOCAUST (LEADING TO THE ATOMIC BOMB)

Early 1800's — Japan first began to open the country to foreign trade.

1868 to 1873 — Japan drifted toward democratic ideas with a parliament but with power in the hands of an emperor.

1889 — Japan created a new constitution, which gave the Emperor power to decide on war or cessation of war.

1894 — Japan had become a military power and had gone to war with China. China had to grant Korea independence, Japan occupied Taiwan, Pescadores Islands, and threatened Liaotung Peninsula (Southern Manchuria).

1904 — Japan (aided by Britain) defeated the Russians; obtained portions of Manchuria, further control of Korea, part of the island of Sakhalin (north of Hokkaido).

1910 — Japan totally annexed Korea, changed name to Chosen.

1918 — Obtained Marshall, Caroline and Mariana Islands, having taken them from Germany during World War I.

1928 — Escalated the war in China.

1928 — **November 10** – Hirohito, upon being crowned Emperor, vowed to "work for world peace."

1931 — Mukden Incident – Using a fake incident, overran all of Manchuria, and made it a Japanese state; expanding their aggression to most of northern China. China identifies this date as a date that will live in infamy (REMEMBER 9/18). It is comparable to the Japanese' treacherous bombing of Pearl Harbor, Hawaiian Islands, December 7, 1941, which date created "Remember Pearl Harbor," the battle slogan of the United States of

America in the Pacific War against Japan.

1932 to 1945 — Col Ishii Shiro created Unit 731, the most diabolical biological and chemical warfare experimental army unit ever. It infected Chinese and other prisoners with myriad diseases, eventually killing thousands in horrible inhuman experiments, continuing until the atomic bomb was dropped, ending the war.

1933 — Japan, a member of the League of Nations, was pressured not to escalate the war in China and not to continue to occupy Manchuria.

1933 — **February 25** – After the League of Nations passed a resolution censuring Japan for continuing its aggression in China, Japan walked out of the League of Nations.

1934 — Pu Yi, former Emperor of China, became puppet Emperor of Manchukno (Manchuria).

1937 — **July** – The China Incident – Japanese troops created a fight with Chinese troops at Marco Polo Bridge, starting a full-scale invasion of China.

1937 — **August** – Japanese bombers from Taiwan and Kyushu bombed Nanking and Shanghai.

1937 — **November** – Imperial General Headquarters created in Tokyo composed of the Emperor, Chiefs of the Army, and Naval General staffs.

1937 — **December** – **Nanking Massacre** – Japan massacred 300,000 Chinese civilian women, men and children in Nanking. While the Nanking massacre is the most prominent in the barbaric rampage of the Japanese, it represents only about one-hundredth of the 30,000,000+ Chinese, Southeast Asians, Filipinos, and Pacific Islanders annihilated by the Japanese military through 1945. Iris Chang thoroughly researched and documented the horrible Nanking Massacre in her book "Rape of Nanking." All people everywhere should honor Iris Chang for her work in giving the world an accurate, historical account of this tragedy. (Note: Iris Chang died in 2004)

1938 — Japan had captured all major Chinese cities.

1938 — Japan proclaimed a new order calling it the "Greater East Asian Co-Prosperity Sphere." (What great prosperity for China, all of Southeast Asia and ultimately the Philippines, Indonesia and preparations for taking Australia. The 30,000,000 killings in China and atrocities by Unit 731, along with the enslavement of Korea and all occupied islands and territories, negated any idea of co-prosperity. The only prosperity, in all these areas, was for the expansion of the cruel Japanese Empire.)

1940 — Japan occupied Indo-China and also joined Germany and Italy as Axis powers. Japan bombed Chungking, the temporary capitol of China, day and night.

1941 — **July** – Japanese troops occupy the remainder of Indo-China.

1941 — **December 7 – Bombing of Pearl Harbor** – Japan with a sneak attack (while their diplomats were pretending to negotiate Pacific problems and trade agreements) attacked the United States Naval Base at Pearl Harbor, Hawaii. This sneak attack by the Japanese naval and air forces killed 2,500 Americans, injured thousands more, sank or damaged eight U.S. battleships and other smaller ships and destroyed over 200 aircraft on the ground.

1941 — **December 7 through early 1942** – The Japanese took Philippines and overran Singapore, Hong Kong, Netherland Indies, New Guinea and almost all islands of the Western Pacific, together with Burma and most of Southeast Asia. After the capture of the Bataan Peninsula and Corregidor (Philippines) the Japanese marched thousands of Americans and Filipinos in the humiliating 12-day Bataan Death March, torturing, bayoneting and killing thousands while proudly flaunting it for the entire world to see.

1941 — **December 8** – United States declared war on Japan.

1942 — **July** – **Battle of Midway** – U.S. Pacific Fleet defeated Japanese fleet, sinking four Japanese carriers and changing the course of the war.

1942 — August through November – Guadalcanal – First of American victories in the island hopping campaigns leading to Japan.

1942 — October – New Georgia captured by U.S.

1943 — November – Tarawa (Gilbert Islands) – U.S. took island in bloody battle.

1944 — January – Kwajalein (Marshall Islands) – Another bloody victory by U.S.

1944 — July – Saipan, Marianas Islands – 30,000 Japanese killed in U.S. capture of this island. 4,300 of Japanese deaths were by suicide. 17,000 U.S. casualties.

1944 — August – Tinian and Guam captured by U.S. with fierce fighting, many casualties.

1944 — October – Peleliu captured by U.S. with many casualties (7,500 + U.S.) 10,000 Japanese killed. Intelligence had predicted a small garrison and little resistance.

1944 — October through July of 1945 – Philippines. With the large group of islands in the Philippines, this vicious campaign caused 80,000 U.S. casualties, with 250,000 Japanese killed and 200.000 Filipinos murdered by the Japanese as they were losing the Philippines.

1945 — March – Iwo Jima secured. 23,000 Japanese killed on this small island. All of these were underground in bunkers, caves, and tunnels. 26,000 U.S. casualties in the worst battle for the Marines in the Pacific.

1945 — June – Okinawa. The last vicious battle before the invasion of the main Japanese islands. The Japanese on Okinawa gave an additional and final preview of what an invasion of the Japanese home islands would be.

The preceding nine island campaigns in which the United States of America forces captured these islands in extremely heavy and bloody fighting led to preparations for "Operation Downfall" the invasion of Japan main islands to begin November 1, 1945. This date would have been D-DAY JAPAN.

1944 — There were continuous "Kill Them All Orders" for prisoners of the Japanese. (1/8/1944 Taiwan Prisoners of War Camp Order is shown in Chapter 20 of this book.) There were standing orders in the entire prisoner of war camps in China and elsewhere to kill all prisoners when the main islands were invaded. Prisoners of war, liberated after the atomic bomb was dropped, all say that their Japanese guards told them they would be killed when the invasion of Japan began. This fact was told specifically to this author by POWs Lester Tenney, Mel Rosen, and Frank Bigelow, among others. Many Chinese were killed under this order, but thousands (maybe millions) were saved from the order by the atomic bomb that ended the war.

1943-1945 — Standard procedure in the last years of the war was to behead all airmen captured over Japan.

1945 — **August 6** – Atom bomb dropped on Hiroshima by Lt. Col. Paul W. Tibbet's B-29, named *Enola Gay*.

1945 — **August 9** – Second atom bomb dropped on Nagasaki.

1945 — **August 15 – V-J DAY – By order of the Emperor, Japan surrendered (after much argument among members of the Supreme War Council).**
THIS SHOULD BE CONSIDERED V-J DAY.

1945 — **September 2 – Formal Surrender by Japan aboard U.S. Battleship *Missouri*.**
This could also be considered V-J DAY.

PROPOSED INVASION OF JAPAN

1945 — **November 1** – D-DAY for the invasion of Japan. The initial assault force of 766,700 to be about five times the size of the 150,00 initial D-Day assault force at Normandy in Europe. Operation Downfall at its peak to involve more than 5,000,000 allied military personnel and assuring casualties for the Allies in the millions and many, many millions for the Japanese. Though the Japanese Imperial Army slaughtered many POWs after the Emperor's surrender and slaughtered many innocent civilians in acts of revenge after the surrender, you will see from excerpts from "Betrayal in High Places" in the main text, that the surrender, by preventing the invasion, saved hundreds of thousands of lives which would be claimed by the vengeance of 900,000 Japanese Army troops in China and 600,000 in the rest of Southeast Asia.

2000 — **May 25** – Japan Prime Minister Yoshiro Mori says, "Japan is a divine country centering on the Emperor."

2001 — **August** – Japanese Prime Minister Koizumi goes to Yasukuni Shrine to honor all Japanese military personnel buried there (shrine includes all those Imperial Army soldiers, who committed the Nanking Massacre and all who slaughtered the millions of Chinese, POWs, and Southeast Asians for over thirty years).

V-J DAY — D-DAY JAPAN. Who cares? The few million World War II survivors and their families, that's who! Who knows? Not 1 out of 100 of the present generation can tell you either date. We are so sensitive to the Japanese (now our friends) that we do not promote true history of World War II and its end. (Sad)

D-DAY JAPAN

JAPAN

The Truth About
the Invasion of Japan,
its War Crimes, and
the Atomic Bomb

Chapter 1
D-Day Japan

D-Day Japan, November 1, 1945 was to be the most horrible day of war in all of history.

D-Day Japan was mercifully cancelled by the atomic bomb on August 6, 1945 and V-J Day, August 15, 1945.

Erasing that D-Day was merciful to millions of people, saving 1,000,000 to 2,000,000 U.S. and Allied lives, and saving up to 20,000,000 Japanese lives (this in the invasion alone). I use the phrase 'invasion alone' as it saved hundreds of thousands of lives not involved in the invasion, in China, Southeast Asia, and the Southwest Pacific Islands.

The anti-bomb crowd does not recognize these figures because they do not understand the invasion plans and defenses. Nor do they want to understand them. In none of the anti-bomb books or articles do they display maps of the invasion scenario, or casualties in all the battles with the Japanese leading up to the D-Day plans.

The MAPS in this book will show clearly the hundreds of thousands, maybe 1,000,000, military and civilian deaths which would occur between August 6, 1945 and November 1, 1945 — D-DAY JAPAN.

Never mentioned by the anti-bomb professors is the fact that 150,000 U.S. Prisoners of War, and some 300,000 other POWs, were to be executed by the Japanese the instant Japan was invaded (See 'Kill All Prisoners' order, and statements by all rescued POWs, quoted later in this text.)

Later chapters of this book will show positively that the Japanese Imperial Army would have slaughtered hundreds of thousands in China, Southeast Asia, and all Pacific islands held by the Japanese.

Proof 'positive' for this is the recording of the slaughter of hundreds of POWs even after the Emperor's surrender rescript.

Cancelling D-Day Japan was extremely merciful.

Chapter 2
Correct Decision

This book will show by uncontroverted facts that the decision by President Harry Truman to authorize the United States of America military personnel to drop the atomic bombs on Hiroshima, Japan on August 6, 1945 and Nagasaki, Japan on August 9, 1945 was not only a 100% proper and correct military decision, but considering all the humanitarian and military circumstances at the time, it was mandated.

There should never be any unfounded statements by latter-day revisionist historians that the use of the atomic bomb was questionable. There was not then, nor is there now, any reasonable argument against the use of the atomic bomb. It was absolutely, unequivocally, without question or doubt, the decision President Harry Truman should have made. He should be forever eulogized and credited with being a great leader.

There is no moral difference between the atomic bomb and any other bomb dropped on any city in World War II. No different than London, Manchester, Birmingham, Liverpool, Berlin, Hamburg, Cologne, Bremen, Shanghai, Nanking, or Manila. Only the magnitude of the Bomb was different.

I am challenged frequently about the thirty million I say were slaughtered by the Japanese during the decades of aggression in China and then Southeast Asia and the Pacific Islands.

The inexcusable laxity of the United States (and China), in not documenting and preserving Japanese Imperial Army atrocities for posterity at the end of World War II is a major factor in our being unable to accurately tally the numbers.

Later research did give us generally accurate figures, which I use. The Foreign Ministry of the Republic of China gives the estimate of 35,000,000, slaughtered by the Japanese Imperial Army.

The Global Alliance to Preserve the History of World War II in Asia estimates the figure as 35,000,000 (a description of the Alliance is in the latter part of this book).

Iris Chang, whose book *Rape of Nanking* was a *New York Times* best seller, acclaimed for her research which uncovered much new information about the Japanese atrocities including the Reverend John Rabe diary which verified all the Nanking atrocities and numbers.

Iris Chang in her speech to the Rape of Nanking Redress Committee Mock Tribunal in 2003 (printed in full later in this book) had accumulated figures to show between 19,000,000 and 35,000,000 killings by the Japanese.

Chapter 3
Japanese Propaganda Motives

T his book will also demonstrate how and why the Japanese leadership has used their glib, self-righteous, deprecating criticism of the
Bomb for over sixty years to practically obliterate from recorded history
their Imperial Army's Super Holocaust in killing some 30,000,000 civilian men, women, children and babies (far outnumbering Germany's
Holocaust) in China, Southeast Asia and the Pacific, prior to and during
World War II, including the most savage, inhuman rampage ever known
on this earth. And that history included the most beastly conduct ever
seen in war — conduct too numerous for this chapter, but beginning with
the indescribable torture of all of our fallen airmen, followed by the beheading of all of them. That hideous obscured conduct also included the
order from the Japanese High Command to execute all of the 150,000
allied prisoners (and up to 300,000 more political and military prisoners
and detainees of other countries) in the event of an invasion.

Chapter 4
A Short Chronology of the War with Japan

The United States was catapulted into World War II on December 7, 1941, after Japan, without warning, began bombing American naval vessels and military installations at Pearl Harbor in Honolulu, Hawaii. Among the vessels and aircraft that were destroyed were five battleships and literally thousands of United States military personnel and civilians.

The Japanese military forces, with direct approval of the Emperor and those in High Command, followed the Pearl Harbor bombing with some four years of the most atrocious, savage and inhuman war crimes ever recorded in history.

The savagery occurred while the Japanese hordes enveloped China, Singapore, Hong Kong, Indo-China, in fact all of Southeast Asia, the Philippines and all Pacific Islands west of the Hawaiian Islands as well as those north of Australia.

Americans began many bloody, deadly, island-hopping campaigns throughout the entire Pacific Ocean and Southeast Asia, which ended when the United States succeeded in capturing the Philippines and Okinawa. Suddenly, America and its Allies found themselves poised on the threshold of the most horrendous invasion that could be imagined. "Operation Downfall" was the code name given for a plan to invade the main islands of Japan.

Instead of launching this plan, some four years after Pearl Harbor (Aug. 6, 1945), the U.S. dropped the first atomic bomb on the city of Hiroshima, Japan; and on August 9, 1945, the second atomic bomb was dropped on Nagasaki, Japan. Approximately 190,000 people were killed in the bombings, and Japan surrendered August 15, 1945, bringing an abrupt end to World War II.

Chapter 5
Japan Prior to Pearl Harbor: The Super Holocaust

In order to understand all of the history surrounding the war with Japan we must understand the Japanese empire prior to World War II.

For more than fifty years prior to World War II, the Japanese had not only occupied Korea, conscripted the men for military service, and enslaved its people, but had also committed untold atrocities against the Korean people, torturing, raping, killing Koreans and almost destroying the entire culture of Korea. They took Korean, Chinese, Malaysian and women of all occupied countries and distributed them as sex slaves, "comfort women," for soldiers in Japan's far-flung military machine. They had invaded China and used China as an experimentation battlefield, and in 1931 the fake Mukden Incident* was used as an excuse to broaden the invasion of China.

Actually they used live Chinese people as a laboratory for inhuman tests, such as tests of poison gas, medical experiments, germ and biological warfare experiments and plague infestation. (See Chapter 8, Unit 731.)

A poorly equipped China, at that time, was subjected to invasion and killings, and, as hard as it is to imagine, the total atrocities inflicted on the Chinese vastly outnumbered the atrocities committed by Nazi Germans. (More on this Super Holocaust in a later chapter.)

The Japanese gloss over their atrocities during the decades prior to World War II with an occasional "broad apology" for their "conduct in Asia"; never for the atrocities in Nanking, all of China, and in

---

*The Mukden incident occurred on September 18, 1931 when a Japanese secret agent planted a bomb under a Japanese owned train. The subsequent explosion gave Japan a justifiable excuse to broaden the war and occupy all of Manchuria.

the Philippines during the early stages of the war. These were more horrible than the initial atrocities where some 70,000 or so Philippine troops were captured on Bataan and annihilated. They slaughtered some 150,000 Filipinos as they were losing the Philippines in the later stages of the war.

Neither have they ever admitted or talked about the horrible Bataan Death March killing thousands of Americans, and, above all, the manner in which they treated the Americans before they killed them. (In another portion of this book it is pointed out that these same savage military soldiers were later designated, honored and enshrined, as kami, or gods, in the Yasukuni Shrine in Tokyo for having been one of those who brought peace to Japan.) The Japanese never, in their history books, specifically point out the millions slaughtered by their military in the name of "opposing colonization" by other countries.

In connection with the Japanese claim of occupying the countries of Asia and the Pacific because of western colonization, anyone interested should talk with Koreans of the period, Chinese of that period, Malaysians, Singapore citizens, Indonesian citizens and citizens of many small and large islands they occupied.

Those people who lived through the Japanese occupation could give historians a most enlightened account of that occupation and the fact that it had nothing to do with western imperialism. Those countries were conquered only for the tremendous ruthless expansionist ambitions of the Japanese.

It is shocking to see the Japanese distort their history so as to never acknowledge the past horrible military history in which they were cruel conquerors of many nations, many islands and many people. Nowhere in their history books, or in current accounts circulating in Japan, do they recognize any of the atrocities occurring in China, Korea and Southeast Asia or the Philippines, or the Bataan Death March.

Particularly, they of course want to forget, and do not record the proper perspective on Pearl Harbor as being a treacherous sneak attack in which the United States of America was a total victim to the extent of the killings of thousands of Americans and the destruction of a large part of our Navy.

It is continually shocking to see intelligent people who are supposedly knowledgeable about modern history who have a distorted idea of war history, and much other history, because the propagandists, mainly the Japanese, are promoting their agenda.

It is almost impossible to find a correct history of the Japanese expansion in all of Asia and China, except in a very few books which I will point out later in this book. That history has been, so far as the Japanese are concerned, **totally obliterated**.

Search all your encyclopedias, reference books, and history books and you will find no account of the atrocious actions of the Japanese Imperial Army. I have a book on major events of the 20th Century and not a line about the vicious era concerning the Japanese Imperial Army. Where are those historically correct professors when history is not only being distorted, but being totally obliterated?

Most Japanese probably want the truth, but the belligerent Samurai, Knights of Bushido extremists are similar to the minority of Germans, the extremists, who claim that the Holocaust never actually happened. There has been a question in the minds of many as to the aggressive agenda of the Jewish people in promoting continuous displays, museums and exhibits concerning the Holocaust.

But in looking at the distortion of other history, it is easy to see that the Holocaust can be and is being totally distorted by a radical few trying to control the history of the ages. It must be kept in perspective as to why the Jewish people are consumed with the idea of making sure mankind never forgets the Holocaust.

The same principle should apply to Japanese history. We continue to reiterate that we are now friends of the Japanese; we want to continue to be friends of the Japanese; however, we will not sit idly by and allow the history of the years prior to World War II, the Japanese domination of tremendous portions of China and much of Asia, and their Super Holocaust, to be obliterated for the sole purpose of giving validity to a distorted historic argument about our use of the atomic bomb, and whether it was appropriate.

Chapter 6
Rebutting Continued Historical Distortions

In the face of so many distorted historical accounts, retired Air Force Brigadier General Paul W. Tibbets has had to defend himself, President Truman and the crew of the *Enola Gay* in dropping the atomic bomb. He needs and deserves complete support from all Americans.

Many Americans continue to be duped by these historical accounts and have some wild, weird sense of over-analyzing the use of the bombs. This book is written in anger over such things as the Hiroshima documentary on Public Television May 27, 1996, which contained poorly researched material described elsewhere in this book.

It was insulting to any member of the armed services who served in the Pacific during World War II along with the millions of military personnel and their families who were being transferred from the horrible war in Europe to face another killing field in which they might have a 50% chance of survival. The ones in the initial landings would have much shorter odds than that.

There were songs and eulogies to the dead and injured of Hiroshima. The Chronicler stated that Americans were left with a raw nerve over Hiroshima; that we have a nuclear entrapment feeling, that we have a denial over the use of the Bomb; and that we need to be liberated from our nuclear entrapment.

This is incorrect and part of the continuing revisionist attempt to get us to feel guilty about the Bomb. On this program, there was a reading of a maudlin speech by an American, Celeste Holmes, quoting the pitiful victims; showing endless pictures of victims. The final irony on the program was that the Mayor Hiraoka had stated in a very condescending manner that we would have to "wait for history" to judge whether the Bomb should have been dropped.

We do not need to wait for history, which is being totally molded and warped by people using some weird philosophy to distort the true history of the war, and the true history behind the atrocious Japanese military war machine, which had dominated China and Asia for decades.

Instead of asking questions about President Truman and the atomic bomb, Americans should be answering all of the questions. Who produced that Public TV program? The Japanese Foreign Ministry? Or the same people who flock to the Yasukuni Shrine?

Public television should produce another program to let some clear thinking Americans present the proper perspective on the Bomb and why we have no reason to have a "raw nerve" or feel "nuclear entrapment."

On a great number of occasions since August 1945, the wisdom of President Harry Truman ordering the use of the atomic bombs has been called into question by the Japanese, of course, or by someone else with an agenda who is too biased to know or examine the facts surrounding its use. Criticism of President Truman and the United States of America (I should emphasize that the United States of America used the Bomb, and that it was on behalf of the United States of America) seemed to intensify during the many fifty-year commemoration programs or projects concerning the end of World War II. The necessity and morality of the decision to use the atomic bomb to end the war was assailed by many in the United States. Many high officials in Japan used the fifty-year commemoration ceremonies in Japan to try to brand the USA as barbaric.

Barbaric![1] How ironic: From a nation that, for over 50 years prior to Pearl Harbor had enslaved Korea, rampages through China, murdering 30,000,000 people in China and Southeast Asia and tortured and murdered our military personnel in the Bataan Death March, after the capture of the Philippines for no other reason than unbridled savagery.

As I will elaborate for you later, the Japanese military had been, and were at the time, the most inhuman force in all of history. Let me repeat, the Japanese military forces who rampaged, almost unchecked, through

---

[1] An unforgivable statistic for the Japanese: 45% of the American prisoners of war held in Japanese concentration camps died, while only 2% or 3% of the prisoners in German concentration camps died. Barbaric?? The Japanese Military gave special attention to the torture and killing of American and other prisoners.

China, Southeast Asia and the Pacific on a Super Holocaust for decades prior to and including World War II, were the most inhuman, barbaric and destructive of human life, in all of history. All of history? Yes.[2]

The Japanese have **no standing** to question the morality or brutality of the atomic bomb.

In short, this Judge does not want the Japanese to be "my conscience" on the use of the atomic bomb, nor are they the ones to go to the Peace Park in Hiroshima every August to be the conscience of the United States or the World on the use of the Bomb.

---

[2]The Nazi Germany extinction of over 6,000,000 Jews in that Holocaust is the most unbelievably cruel barbaric and inhuman attempt at the elimination of a race of people in all history.

Chapter 7
The Super Holocaust

There is no desire to detract from or minimize, the terrible German Nazi Holocaust in killing some six million (6,000,000) Jews.

But, with that being a Holocaust, how do we designate a Japanese reign of terror for over three decades in which probably five times as many people were executed and with many of these thirty million (30,000,000) or so executions being preceded by torture so diversified as to numb the thoughts of all humanity? For example: throwing a Filipino baby in the air and bayoneting it as it falls, dissecting U.S. Airmen alive, and preserving their remains in formaldehyde, cutting open prisoners while alive, cutting off women's breasts and children's arms while alive. Add cannibalism, with the Japanese known to have eaten meat, liver and other body parts of beheaded prisoners. Some killed for the express purpose of cannibalism (*Flyboys* by James Bradley, page 284).

I think we can call it a Super Holocaust.

Chapter 8
Proposed Smithsonian *Enola Gay* Exhibit: A National Disgrace

The culmination of fifty years of propaganda concerning the atomic bomb (as opposed to the true recording of historic events involving millions of World War II deaths) occurred during the 50th Anniversary Exhibit to be placed in the National Air and Space Museum. The main part of the Exhibit was to be the *Enola Gay*, the B-29 Superfortress which dropped the first atomic bomb on Hiroshima, August 6, 1945. The title of the exhibit was to be "Crossroads: The End of World War II, the Atomic Bomb and the Origins of the Cold War." This exhibit, as proposed by the National Air and Space Museum, was to only show the nose cone of the *Enola Gay* and was one of the most repulsive (to Americans) exhibits imaginable. It was a special insult to military personnel in all of World War II, and was an insult to the intelligence of the American public; that is, except to the few Revisionists who, I feel, had no sense of correct history and that were headed by Martin O. Harwit, the Director of the Smithsonian Air and Space Museum.

This exhibit was dominated by photographs of the suffering Japanese and the horrors of the atomic bombs dropped on Hiroshima and Nagasaki. (No one would argue with the immediate horror of these two bombs and at no time has the United States sought to diminish the awful destructive power of the bombs.) The glaring insults of the exhibit were spotlighted by one of the worst phrases one could use about the Pacific War, and I quote: "For most Americans, this was a war of vengeance. For most Japanese, it was a war to defend their unique culture against western imperialism."

Historically, nothing could be further from the truth. Here is Japan, starting a war with a sneak attack on the United States of America (killing thousands of its military personnel and civilians) and who is depicted as only defending its "unique culture."

A shocking revelation came from the curator of the exhibit, Michael J. Neufield, when he stated that a discussion of probable United States casualties during the proposed invasion of Japan or rather the eminent invasion of Japan, was not "historically relevant" to President Truman's decision to drop the Bomb.

Now just let that sink in a moment. It does not matter how many Americans would die in an invasion, the Bomb to prevent it should not have been dropped. What deep thinkers we had at the National Air and Space Museum.

Very notable in the exhibit was the eulogizing of Kamikaze pilots, as being heroes. Kamikaze pilots who were so fanatical as to commit suicide by diving into American warships, in devotion to their Sun God Emperor, do not qualify as heroes, when they were totally indiscriminate, and who dove into a navy hospital ship, the USS *Solace*, killing six nurses for the glory of Japan. What heroes!

Eighty-one members of Congress expressed their total disagreement at the exhibit and tried to remind the Smithsonian of the charter: "The Smithsonian Institution shall commemorate and display the contributions made by the military forces of the nation toward creating, developing and maintaining a free peaceful and independent society and culture of the United States. The valor and sacrificial service of men and women of the armed forces shall be portrayed as an inspiration to the present and future generations." As expected, the Veterans of Foreign Wars, the American Legion and the Air Force Association were appalled at the proposed exhibit, and pointed out that the Japanese were depicted as victims, despite their decades of aggression, atrocities and brutalities against American and Allied civilians and military personnel, and in spite of their history of having killed some 30,000,000 people in China, Southeast Asia and the Pacific Theater in a tremendous Asian and China Holocaust.

Another astounding occurrence was disclosed when it was revealed that no input had been asked from Veterans Associations, or from knowledgeable military historians concerning the exhibit, or from the Air Force.

It was shockingly disclosed that the Smithsonian National Air and Space Museum staff had "Federal Expressed" the script of the proposed exhibit asking for a quick response from the Japanese, seeking their input.

Even more shocking was that no input was sought from any Veterans of World War II or any American military organization for the exhibit. The Japanese had no right to dictate any of the terms of this exhibit.

The Veterans of Foreign Wars, American Legion, Air Force Association and also a six-member review team was composed as follows: Brigadier General William M. Constantine, USAF (Ret.), volunteer NASM Docent and Team Chairman; Colonel Thomas Alison, USAF (Ret.) NASM Curator for Military Aviation; Dr. Gregg Herken, Historian and Chairman, NASM Department of Space History; Colonel Donald Lopez, USAF (Ret.), former NASM Deputy Director and Senior Advisor Emeritus; Kenneth Robert, NASM volunteer Docent; and Dr. Steven Soter, Special Assistant to the Director, NASM and Team Secretary. The review team attempted to work out a reasonable solution for the presentation of the exhibit that would be fair historically. However, after considerable effort by the knowledgeable review team and also after several exhibit changes, Martin Harwit continued to be arbitrary.

Director Martin Harwit, Director of the National Air and Space Museum, arbitrarily fixed 63,000 as the maximum casualty loss, which he would put in the exhibit as the number of Allied casualties anticipated in the event of an invasion of Japan, to compare against the casualties in the Hiroshima and Nagasaki bombs. As opposed to the 63,000 that he finally determined to use, after negotiation, Harwit and his NASM Directors had originally stated in the proposed exhibit that the Allies would only have 25,000 casualties in an invasion of Japan. How BIZARRE!

Although the Veterans of Foreign Wars, American Legion and Air Force Association were continually willing to work in good faith to make the exhibit historically correct, the Smithsonian, rather than reach any reasonable compromise on the exhibit, cancelled the exhibit January 30, 1995.

The PhD's at the National Air and Space Museum must have had some deep-seated dislike for American military personnel or American Armed Services, or a decided anti-American political correctness bias, to want to form this exhibit into some pasquinade directed at those military personnel who mercifully ended the war, led by a great President, Harry Truman.

How dare these people, entrusted with our National Air and Space Museum take it upon themselves to try to anathematize President Harry Truman, and all the others who had a part in that glorious event!

Brigadier General Paul Tibbets, Jr. (retired) and all the others who rode with them should not have to defend that event every August 6th. We ought to lead a memorial service for and with them, each August 6th, and we should insulate them from criticism by our entire populace proclaiming that what they did was correct, and approved, and have none of the revisionist agenda each year, adding to the questioning of the decision to drop the bomb. The *Enola Gay* should have been enshrined (in full) at that time, in the National Air and Space Museum with commentary by appropriate patriotic Americans selected by congress and not by some politically correct professors.

Why should servicemen and citizens of our World War II era and those who went through the Pacific War have to listen to such inappropriate criticism each August, and why would all of the World War II veterans and for that matter, Veterans of all of our wars, have to wonder why any American would be more concerned with the people who died at Hiroshima or Nagasaki than the hundreds of thousands of his buddies who were casualties in the Pacific, and useless casualties at that? And why would we have to be wondering why Americans, or any other countries would be more concerned with the people who died at Hiroshima or Nagasaki than the additional millions who would have died in an invasion of Japan if the bomb had not been used?

If accounts of World War II continue in the present direction, the Japanese will have future generations believing the Pearl Harbor sneak attack was a defensive maneuver to keep the United States fleet from entering Tokyo Bay, and that it was necessary to cripple or sink most of our Pacific fleet in the name of anti-colonialism. Have any accounts by the Japanese rulers, or Japanese historians, acknowledged that the sneak attack on Pearl Harbor was wrong or bad? They will occasionally, in a backhanded way, say they "regret the war in the Pacific" (only because it brought destruction to their conquering military aspirations).

This claim about the Japanese only being interested in fighting "to defend their **unique culture against western imperialism,**" when coming from an American, can only come from a writer who has distorted anti-nuclear feelings. *All of us, with any common sense, have anti-nuclear feelings.* This proper exhibiting of the *Enola Gay* certainly would not be to promote nuclear warfare, or to aggrandize nuclear warfare. The exhibit should be a factual occurrence of what happened at the end of World War II, and the airplane that was the symbol of the ending of World War II. As far as nuclear power is concerned, no official of the United States, nor leaders of its military, have ever expressed any other desire than that there should be no nuclear proliferation.

The proposed *Enola Gay* exhibit could not be explained from any reasonable standpoint. The exhibit "the Final Act: The Atomic Bomb and the End of World War II" was explained by some writers as an attempt to bridge the gap between pre-atomic and atomic age youths and the rest of U.S. citizenry. They suggested that there was a typical split between those of the World War II generation and those 40 and 50 years later. There should be no split between those of our age during World War II, those of the Korean War era, those of the Vietnam era, those 50 years later and those 1,000 years later. That is, if history had been recorded properly and if the maudlin bleeding hearts had not taken over the writing of history and repeating over and over that the bomb was questionable, and repeating over and over that it was not necessary, and repeating over and over that it was barbaric. None of that is true. It should not be controversial; it should not ever be referred to as barbaric, should never be referred to as questionable. It was a correct, great, right, military, (humanitarian, if you will) decision which future American generations should never have to apologize for or defend.

John Correll was the Editor-in-Chief of the *Air Force Magazine* at the time of the *Enola Gay* controversy. When the activists continued to criticize the *Enola Gay* exhibit and those who had helped to change it to a more reasonable exhibit, John Correll wrote a number of good articles on the controversy and in one of these "The Activists and the *Enola Gay*" he itemized, in an excellent treatise, just how wrong and untenable the argument of the activists were.

The controversy over the exhibit spotlights a glaring defect in the Smithsonian Institution, particularly the National Air and Space

Museum. I question how we could put Revisionists, with an agenda to mold the minds of future generations, in positions of authority such as Directors of the National Air and Space Museum?

This group of "historians" were trying to give their 'enlightened' modern spin to their anti-nuclear agenda. That Harwit and his PhD's (Doctorate Professors) were almost able to take upon themselves the real distorted molding of the history of the end of World War II in the most visited Museum on earth, is frightening.

During the controversy over the proposed *Enola Gay* exhibit, two authors who were writing a book critical of the dropping of the atomic bomb wrote to the *New York Times* "it has never been easy to reconcile dropping the Bomb with ourselves as decent people." They blame the lack of an impartial examination of the Bomb on "misleading official explanations and government secrecy." This is poor journalism because the American people, or the government, have never made any misleading statements about the use of the atomic bomb, and there has been no government secrecy about the Bomb.

While readers need to know the extent to which the Professors at NASM and their supporters would go to show the U.S.A. as wrong in dropping the atomic bomb, they also need to know the final journey of the *Enola Gay*.

Years after the original 1995 fiasco, in 2003 the *Enola Gay* was reassembled in its entirety at the Steven Udvar-Hazy Center Museum at Dulles Airport west of Washington.

The exhibit described how the bomber was such an improvement over other bombers at that time, and states: "On August 6, 1945, this Martin-built B-29-45-M0 dropped the first atomic weapon used in combat on Hiroshima, Japan."

The primary focus shows that it was the most advanced aircraft in the world. No opinion on the use of the Bomb is expressed.

This exhibit was opened over the renewed howls of "Committee for a National Discussion of Nuclear History and Current Policy," comprised of the same group who were supportive of the original proposed (flawed) *Enola Gay* exhibit, viz: Peter Kuznick, Robert Jay Lifton, Hiroshima Mayor Tadatoshi Akiba, Julian Bond, Kai Bird, Norman Lear and over one hundred other political activists.

The exhibit shows that we are still too sensitive to Japanese feelings to say, "We bombed you to save lives, ours and yours."

This author believes that we should not hesitate to correctly show the atom bomb casualties (as Kuznick, Mayor Akiba, Alperovitz and the "Committee" want) but also show the millions of lives *saved* by the Bomb.

The activists and NASM professors have all fallen in line with the Japanese propaganda trying to make us feel guilty about the Bomb.

We are not guilty.

We do not feel guilty.

We don't want anyone to tell us that we should feel guilty.

We don't want anyone to reflect on our decency for dropping the Bomb.

Thinking Americans have a clear conscience about the Bomb. This revisionism is some 'crazy political correctness' that has come about by distorted thinking, derived from fifty years of Japanese propaganda, in trying to divert attention from the most horrible atrocities known to mankind, by the Japanese, prior to and during World War II.

We all hope that the dropping of the Bomb will be a deterrent to anyone starting a nuclear war; it has been to this point.

The atomic bomb has neither started nor participated in any war since its sole use in ending World War II.

Chapter 9
Truman's Decision

The first of August, 1945, President Harry Truman knew that he was mandated to order the dropping of the atomic bomb on Japan. There was an invasion plan, OPERATION DOWNFALL (First Phase being Operation Olympic, the Invasion of Kyushu Island), which was scheduled for November 1, 1945 to begin the invasion of the main Japanese islands (the Second Phase being Operation Coronet, the invasion of Honshu Island, to begin March 1, 1946). The invasion at its height would involve more than 5,000,000 Allied military personnel, most being those of the United States of America.

President Truman knew that defending against any invasion were 2,300,000* Japanese regular troops, supplemented by another 4,000,000 army and navy personnel in a militia type organization, twenty-five million people in addition (women, men and children) were mustered to supplement all of these defenders.

He knew that they were pledged to "fight to the death" in defense of the Emperor and the homeland. He also knew of the history of the previous four years in which the American and Allied forces had reached this point in the Pacific War. The President had to analyze previous battles with the Japanese and the casualties from those battles. Beginning with the bloody battle of Guadalcanal in which so many American lives were taken and in which there was never any surrender by the Japanese, he then continued one by one analyzing the different island campaigns to see exactly what occurred by numbers.

---

*Note: In the three-month period of Aug., Sept. and Oct. leading up to Nov. 1, 1945, the invasion date, the number of regular Japanese troops would increase dramatically as many thousands were being brought back from China and Southeast Asia to defend the homeland. The number of regular troops could be expected to reach 3,000,000 by Nov. 1, 1945.

One only needs to spotlight about five of the last campaigns in the Pacific to realize what President Harry Truman knew would be the results of an invasion of Japan. In naming some five campaigns, these authors do not mean to detract from, or belittle the importance of, nor the savage defense of, any particular territory by the Japanese, nor the heroic efforts of the United States and Allied troops in "stepping stones" across the Pacific Isles (Guadalcanal, Tarawa etc.) to get to the place where the Allies found themselves on August 1, 1945. Likewise, great heroic efforts in the Southeast Asia, China and Indonesian theaters and all other areas cannot be forgotten. These listed campaigns will show that casualties would be tremendous in the invasion of Japan.

Mariana Islands

The Mariana Islands began with the invasion of Saipan, June 15, 1944 with the island being secured July 9, 1944. Nearby Tinian was secured August 1, 1944 and the island of Guam was invaded July 21, 1944 and secured by Americans on August 10, 1944. On Saipan alone, the United States incurred some 17,752 casualties. The Japanese incurred some 25,000 to 30,000 deaths of which 4,300 Japanese died in suicide charges against the United States troops after Saipan was, in effect, secured. Their commander, Japanese Lieutenant General Yoshitsugi Saito, committed suicide after telling his troops to follow him: he was "going to seek out the enemy."

Accounting for 4,300 of the Japanese losses on Saipan, was the suicide charge against our troops, and many Japanese leaping off the cliffs from the northern end of Saipan in senseless suicide (or do the Japanese claim these were meaningful?).

An interesting note for movie-goers; Lee Marvin of Hollywood fame, "Dirty Dozen," "Paint Your Wagon," "The Man Who Shot Liberty Valance," "Cat Ballou" and many others, was in the U.S. Marine Corps, having been on a number of invasions prior to Saipan; and on Saipan, of 247 Marines in I Company, 4th Marine Regiment, 4th Marine Division, only he and five others survived. He was wounded and evacuated on the hospital ship "Solace" and spent thirteen months hospitalized. The "Solace" was later the victim, along with its nurses and medical personnel, of a Kamikaze attack (described later in this book), by one of the Emperor's kamikaze "heroes."

On Tinian almost all of the Japanese were killed because of their resistance and determination to die for the Emperor. The United States had some 1,800 casualties on Tinian. On Guam, the United States casualties were approximately 7,000 and very few Japanese surrendered on Guam, although because of the dense jungle on Guam many Japanese went into the hills and jungles of Guam and survived for a long period of time. Many did not ever surrender even after the surrender of the high command in Japan. (That will be touched on in another chapter.)

Peleliu Island

The next brutal campaign after Guam was the battle of Peleliu. This battle began on September 15, 1944, and the island was declared secured on October 12, 1944. In this battle it was predicted that it would require only two days to complete and while the island may have been declared secure on October 12, 1944, there were not only deadly skirmishes which continued for quite some time, but, as will be pointed out later, some of the Japanese stayed in caves for a long time after the island had been declared secure and quite a lengthy time after the Japanese high command had surrendered in Japan, and the war was over.

This brutal campaign cost the United States 8,387 casualties and of the 10,695 Japanese originally on the island, all were killed except 301 who were captured. The tenacity of the Japanese on Peleliu was, as in all of these islands, unrelenting, and they were determined to kill as many United States personnel as possible, knowing that they would be killed if they did not surrender, and they had no idea of surrendering.

Again, faced with the absolute knowledge that they would be annihilated, the entire Japanese garrison fought to the end with no hope of winning this battle.

Listen to a man I consider the "Ultimate Marine," who fought on Peleliu and gives us for this book, an insight into what the Japanese home island invasion would be like.

"On Peleliu Island we encountered the first of those Japanese homeland types of defenses in depth where the defenders were ordered to fight until killed in their positions.

The Japanese had been on Peleliu since seizing it from the

Germans after World War I. Under the high ridges were five levels of caves. Cannons from sunken ships were in the mouths of caves with steel doors which opened when they were ready to fire. Machine guns forty feet back in caves fired bursts out of small apertures.

Their efforts at fortification were concealed by heavy jungle foliage and by removing local natives from the island.

Our limited efforts at reconnaissance failed to detect the defenses, leading our senior commanders to announce a "cake walk, all over in two days." We were in the middle of these heavy defenses soon after landing. Our division lost 6,000 casualties in the first four days. Each Japanese defender "killed Americans until he, himself, was killed."

— General Ray Davis

In line with the comments of General Davis concerning the "Cake Walk," it should be noted that the bombardment of Peleliu had ceased before the Marine landing, as the battleships and cruisers had proclaimed that there were "no more significant targets to be shelled." The Marines found the hidden defenses to be almost without damage when they went on Peleliu.

General Raymond Davis, U.S. Marine Corps (Retired), received the Navy Cross, Purple Heart and other medals for his part in Peleliu. He also fought on Guadalcanal, Korea where he received the Medal of Honor for the Chosin Reservoir battle, and Vietnam. He was later appointed Assistant Commandant of the U.S. Marine Corps.

Iwo Jima Island

The next campaign was the brutal one for Iwo Jima. It began February 19, 1945 and the island was declared secured March 26, 1945. Statistically, this was the worst for the United States of any of the battles. It involved some 71,245 Marines ready to take the island. 10,087 Marines, Navy personnel, Navy doctors, Corpsmen and other personnel (3,266) were killed with a total of 26,038 casualties on Iwo Jima. Of the 23,000 Japanese on the island, all except 215 were killed, these being the only ones taken prisoner. It was not the aim of the Japanese to ever be taken prisoner, but to die for the Emperor and the homeland, and to kill as many as possible for the Emperor.

A very significant part of the Iwo Jima battle was the fact that for some 2 ½ months before the marines invaded Iwo Jima, the island was under constant air and naval bombardment. Naval bombardment from battleships, their sixteen-inch guns and cruiser bombardment, and from air bombardment is a disastrous occurrence on an island of this size; some five miles long. Yet with all of this bombardment the Japanese had a complete garrison holed up in bunkers, caves and tunnels to oppose the Marines at the time of their landing.

The terrible statistics of Iwo Jima certainly illustrate what would occur on any invasion of Japan as their mindset was to kill as many Americans as possible before they all were certainly to be killed.

The Philippines

This campaign began in the last part of 1944 and, with such a huge group of large islands, it continued until July of 1945. The United States incurred some 80,000 casualties in the Philippine campaign.

While the Philippine campaign was no less vicious on the part of the Japanese in fighting to the death, one of the more significant and horrifying features of this campaign was that, as the Japanese were being defeated and their capture or withdrawal in the Philippines, and particularly in Manila, was eminent, they slaughtered 200,000 Filipinos as a barbaric final act in the Philippines.

This gives a vivid illustration as to what the Japanese homeland islands would be like for all of those prisoners there and elsewhere in the Japanese prisoner of war camps. At Leyte the Japanese sacrificed their entire garrison of over 50,000. The magnitude of their losses here was huge.

Another gruesome occurrence was brought to light when survivors in the Philippines stated that on December 14, 1944, Japanese guards herded 150 Americans into bunkers used for air raid shelters, threw gasoline and blazing torches on them, and when the screaming victims tried to escape, they were bayoneted or machine-gunned. This is a true account by some survivors.

The Philippine campaign saw the first use of the Kamikaze, or suicide airplane by the Japanese. A pilot wishing to sacrifice his life for the Emperor would dive his airplane into a ship or military installation seeking only to kill as many Americans as he could as he plunged to his death.

Okinawa

Okinawa involved an island south of the mainland of Japan and this campaign was on an island some sixty miles long and two to eighteen miles wide. Some 550,000 United States military personnel were involved in the operation, and it resulted in 68,000 casualties to the United States. For the Japanese, practically all of their defense forces, 80,000 regular troops and 20,000 of the home defense were killed, leaving only a very few captured. A startling figure from this campaign was that 150,000 civilians were killed during this operation. A great number of these civilian casualties were not from bombardment or from casual gunfire on both sides, but a great number were used mercilessly by the Japanese, sending them toward the American lines at night to draw fire, and also sending them to explode hidden mines.

Again the Japanese fought with only one thing in mind, to kill as many as possible before they were defeated; they knew that their defeat, and death, was inevitable.

The invasion of Okinawa involved four army and two Marine divisions. It was comparable to the Normandy landing with the original assault totaling 150,000 men. There was a 1,300 ship fleet in the operation. Army and Marine forces had 68,000 casualties.

The Okinawa battle also demonstrated in a more far-reaching and deadly manner how the Japanese would use the kamikaze (suicide) planes. The air attacks exceeded anything previously encountered from the Japanese, being so close to Japan – only 350 miles. The Japanese committed 6,000 plus aircraft to the battle, of which 3,000 were kamikazes. Thirty-five United States Navy ships were sunk and 350 ships were damaged, **with the United States Navy suffering more casualties than the combined total of all its previous wars.**

Dec. 7, 1941 Attack on Pearl Harbor	Japanese Defense Forces Aug. 1945
Pearl Harbor	**Regular Army**
Sneak attack by Japanese on Pearl Harbor killing 2,500 Americans, and injuring thousands.	(By Nov. 1, 1945 Regular Army would be 3,000,000)
8 U.S. Battleships were sunk or damaged, and over 200 aircraft were destroyed on the ground.	2,300,000 Regular Army 4,000,000 Army-Navy (Militia Type)
Pearl Harbor is approximately 5,000 miles from Japan.	25,000,000 (organized men, women and children)

Map of the Central and Northwest Pacific Ocean

Island Campaigns and Battle Information Showing Dates and Casualties Leading to the Invasion of the Home Islands of Japan

Hawaiian Islands

Midway Island

Honolulu

Wake Island

Ocean

Marshall Islands

Kwajalein

esia

Gilbert Islands

Tarawa

Note: proportion and position of some islands may have been altered slightly to fit all information on map.

June 1942
Naval Battle of
Midway Island
U.S. fleet sank 4 Japanese
Aircraft cariers changing the
course of the war.

July 9, 1944
Saipan
14 miles long, 2-4 miles wide
Japanese - 20,000 killed
(4,300 Japanese suicides)
U.S.A. - 1,800 casualties

Aug. 10, 1944
Guam
31 miles long, 8 miles wide
Japanese - 10,000 killed
U.S.A. - 7,000 casualties

Aug. 10, 1944
Tinian
12 miles long, 2-6 miles wide
Japanese - 4,000 killed
U.S.A. - 1,800 casualties

Oct. 12, 1944
Peleliu
5 miles long and ½ mile wide
Japanese - 10,500 killed
U.S.A. - 8,387 casualties

March 26, 1945
Iwo Jima
4 ½ miles long, 2 miles wide
Japanese - 23,000 killed
U.S.A. - 26,038 casualties

Oct. 1944-July 1945
The Philippines
200,000 Filipinos murdered by
Japanese
Japanese - 250,000 killed
U.S.A. - 80,000 casualties

June 22, 1945
Okinawa
60 miles long, 2-18 miles wide
Japanese - 100,000 killed
Marine & Army - 68,000
casualties (U.S. Navy - more
casualties than all previous
wars combined)
35 U.S. Navy ships sunk
350 ships damaged
150,000 civilian deaths

Operation Downfall
Master Invasion Plan
Nov. 1, 1945
20,000 Naval Vessels
Aircraft Carriers, Battleships, Cruisers, Destroyers,
Landing Crafts, Assault Crafts, etc.
Total U.S.A. and Allied Personnel Involved in the
Invasion: Approximately 5,000,000

Lessons Learned

These five campaigns taught us the following five things:

1. **The Japanese would not surrender just by being over-whelmed in battle.** They had no chance of winning, or even of survival, on Okinawa, Iwo Jima, Peleliu, Saipan, or Tinian. Many would hide in the jungles of Guam or the Philippines, but none surrendered because of imminent defeat.

2. **As General Ray Davis described; we saw what their "homeland types of defense" would be.** "We knew with the resources and personnel in the main Japanese islands being devoted to building bunkers, pill-boxes, endless tunnels and traps and their resolve to stay in these hidden caves and defenses to their death, that casualties would far exceed those horrible ones previously experienced." According to General Davis and others, "when viewed after the Japanese surrender", the intricate death traps and defenses on Kyushu, Shikoku and Honshu were even more deadly than previously thought.

3. **The Kamikaze aircraft the Japanese had in reserve would inflict frightful damage from ship to shore (up to 16,000 of these).**

4. **Civilian deaths could be in the range of 20 million.** There would be no slaughter of civilians by the Japanese, as in the Philippines, but the 150,000 civilian deaths on Okinawa told much about what deaths would be on the main Japanese islands, with some 75,000,000 inhabitants at the time.

5. **Allied casualties would be numbered in the millions using any reasonable analysis of the Okinawa and other campaigns.**

With the Okinawa, Iwo Jima, Saipan, Tinian, Guam, Peleliu and Philippine casualty figures before him, President Truman examined the preparation for invasion of Kyushu, Operation Olympic, set for November 1, 1945.

The map, shown on pages 58-59, will graphically show the figures involved in this invasion.

Early intelligence estimates beginning in mid-1944 had fixed the number of Japanese troops defending Kyushu at 100,000 and, by April 1945 was thought to be 246,000 and that the Japanese could add roughly 100,000 more army troops by November 1, 1945. (Signals Intelligence Monograph (CIA) page 6.) In a June 18 meeting, General Marshall and the Joint War Plans committee, with Intelligence available to them, had predicted, and expressed to the President, that Japanese forces moving to reinforce Kyushu would be "cut to a trickle if not choked off entirely."

Not only were the reinforcements of Japanese on Kyushu not cut off, but July 29, 1945, Ultra (Magic) intercepts show that three additional combat divisions have arrived on Kyushu with two more enroute. (Signals Intelligence Monograph, page 19.) Quite dramatic (startling) is a look at Document 11 of Signals Intelligence Monograph of July 21, 1945 from Ultra intercepts showing Japanese strength on Kyushu at 455,000 and a comparison with Document 15 on July 26, 1945 (ONLY SIX DAYS LATER), showing an increase of 70,000 troops to 525,000 with an additional army division en route. This has the total Japanese troops for Kyushu approaching 600,000 by the time of the atomic bomb and still rising, with the invasion date of November 1, 1945 still three months off.

The estimates of 500,000 casualties were becoming very obsolete.

With this scenario, President Truman returned from the Potsdam Conference (Stalin, Churchill, Truman) and, on July 27, 1945 the Potsdam Declaration (cited at the end of this book) was sent to the Japanese with the ultimatum to unconditionally surrender "all armed forces" of Japan, or the allies were poised to strike the final blows upon Japan. (*Codename Downfall*, page 325.)

Premier Suzuki, July 28, 1945, at a press conference, said that Japan would "mokusatsu" it, as it was of "no great value."

"Mokusatsu" could be translated several ways, such as "treat with silent contempt" or "to be silent - to kill." U.S. diplomats interpreted "mokusatsu" as "unworthy of public notice" and as a rejection. (*Codename Downfall*, page 326.)

Gar Alperovitz and the other revisionists make a big issue of the fact that U.S. officials should have known the word was ambiguous; it could mean "to kill with silence," "take no notice of" or "withhold comment."

(Author's note: "withhold comment" is a unique creation of Gar Alperovitz and found in no other source of which I am aware.)

In *The Last Great Victory* Stanley Weintraub, page 289 lists four translations of "mokusatsu": "ignore entirely," "regard as unworthy of notice," "kill with silence," or "treat with silent contempt." Weintraub says that Ultra (Magic) intercepts shows the 'all or nothing' military prevailed over the moderates.

Totally destroying Alperovitz' (Revisionists) claim that we should have tried to look behind the 'mokusatsu' word, is the fact that Suzuki added that Japan would keep on fighting until the war was won. (*Codename Downfall*, page 326.)

Though no other confirmation of the fact Suzuki was rejecting the Potsdam Proclamation is needed, the Japanese official news agency DOMEI translated "mokusatsu" as "ignore." (*Enola Gay* by Thomas & Witts, page 232.) In *The Last Great Victory* by Stanley Weintraub (page 288) says DOMEI News Agency quoted Suzuki specifically: "I believe the Joint Proclamation by the three countries is nothing but a rehash of the Cairo Declaration. As for the Government, it does not find any important value in it, and there is no other recourse but to ignore it entirely, and resolutely fight for the successful conclusion of the war."

Weintraub points out, as have others, that Japan could have made overtures to the United States through neutral countries if it wanted to discuss the Potsdam Proclamation. (See also *Japan's Decision to Surrender* by Butow P. 145)

Japanese-run *Hong Kong News* published a "censored" Potsdam Proclamation with a headline "Don't Scare Us." The ultimatum, it declared, was a piece of unqualified impudence. (*The Last Great Victory*, page 271.)

While Premier Suzuki's "mokusatsu" and stated rejections of the Potsdam Ultimatum overwhelm all claims by revisionists (Nitze and the others) of an "early surrender" claim, there are other undisputed facts that we know proved beyond question—NO EARLY SURRENDER.

The last months of the War, Japan's Supreme War Council, known as the Big Six, determined absolutely whether and how to end the war.

This council was composed of Premier Admiral Baron Kantaro Suzuki, Navy Minister Admiral Yonai, Foreign Minster Shigenori Togo, War Minister General Anami, Chief of the Army General Staff General

Manoru Umezu, and Chief of the Naval General Staff Admiral Toyoda.

While the reader must understand that the ruling Japanese Cabinet of about fourteen, along with a few others (among them: Prince Konoye, Marquis Koichi Kido, Mamoru Shigemitsu, Hisatsume Sacomiyu, Baron Hiranuma) all had influence on the surrender decision, the ultimate decision for recommendation to the Emperor was by the Big Six.

Though one might assume that the Emperor would just decide what to do, that did not, and could not, occur with the military being dominant in Japan.

The Supreme Council had received the Potsdam Proclamation on July 27, 1945 and were still debating it August 10, 1945 even after the second atomic bomb was dropped on Nagasaki, August 9, 1945. (See Butow—*Japan's Decision to Surrender*, page 166 et. Seq.— *Codename Downfall,*" by Allen and Polmar, page, 332 et. Seq.— Weintraub *The Last Great Victory*, page 504 et. seq.)

The Supreme Council was supposed to achieve unanimity before bringing anything to the attention of the Emperor. If the cabinet could not agree or reach a compromise, the cabinet was expected to resign. Since the Emperor was not an arbiter or referee but a silent partner, presenting him with a divided opinion was out of the question (Butow—P. 167).

Not discussed, or mentioned, by Nitze, Alperovitz, Kuznick, et al. is the fact that the Supreme War Council, from the time of receiving the Potsdam proclamation July 27, 1945, was divided three to three over acceptance of the proclamation under any conditions until the morning of August 10, 1945.

All of the Big Six had agreed that the Emperor's position had to be preserved or no surrender. They were not sure if the proclamation allowed retention of the Emperor.

However, General Anami, General Umezu and Admiral Toyoda all held out, demanding three other conditions before accepting the proclamation. These three other conditions were as follows: (1) No occupation of Japan; (2) Disarmament and demobilization be left in Japanese hands; (3) War criminals be tried by Japanese tribunals.

Obviously such conditions could not be granted by the allies.

This was the situation right up until the early morning of August 10, 1945.

Premier Suzuki had convinced the Big Six to allow the Emperor to convene an Imperial Conference late on the night of August 9, 1945.

After listening to the indecision of the Big Six, the Emperor, in a lengthy speech, "gave his sanction to the proposal (by Suzuki, Togo and Yonai) to accept the allied proclamation on the basis outlined by the Foreign Minister."

While the Supreme War Council (Big Six) were then committed to accepting the surrender terms, they sent Japan's first surrender offer August 10, 1945, which sought assurance that the Emperor would remain. August 11, 1945 Secretary of State Byrnes' reply made clear that "the authority of the Emperor and the Japanese government to rule shall be subject to the Supreme Commander of the allied powers." (Appendix E.)

Anami, Umezu and Toyoda were still not satisfied, but at the final Imperial Conference on August 14, 1945 the Emperor expressed himself finally that they accept the Potsdam proclamation and "prepare at once an Imperial Rescript for him to broadcast to the nation." This Imperial Rescript of August 14, 1945 announced to the Japanese people that Japan was accepting the provisions of the Joint Declaration of the allies.

In the meantime, on August 11, 1945 a small group of army staff officers committed themselves to staging a coup d'état to prevent the surrender. The attempted coup was led by a Major Hatanaka, who assassinated Lieutenant General Mori because he failed to join the coup group. While the coup groups created chaos for a while, the determination of General Anami and General Umezu to suppress the coup was successful and they terminated it by August 14, so that it did not prevent the surrender announcement. (Butow—*Japan's Decision*, page 210.)

General Anami committed seppuku (hara-kiri) on August 14, 1945 after he and General Umezu had stopped the uprising.

After the Emperor's announcement to the Japanese people, President Truman announced to the United States and the world, that Japan had surrendered and the formal documents of surrender were signed September 2, 1945 aboard the U.S. battleship, the USS *Missouri*.

Chapter 10
Revisionists vs. Truman and the Truth

During the 50-year anniversary of the dropping of the atomic bombs, the mayor of Nagasaki, during a so-called peace program, said, "let history decide whether the atomic bomb was correct."

If we let these idiotic sayings go unanswered, and if we wait until all involved in World War II and the dropping of the Bomb (and really those with the only true perspective) are gone, and let the Japanese and Harwit, Kuznick, Alperovitz and the others continue to distort World War II and the atomic bomb, and Japanese history, the Japanese will have determined "history" for all time.

The Japanese are trying to reverse our roles as aggressor and victim in the Pacific War by constantly hammering at the atomic bomb. We should never let these people write history for us.

Bruce Lee in *Marching Orders* wrote, "According to Karen van Wolferen, who is considered one of the best Western experts on Japan, 'No country has ever spent as much on officially recorded lobbying expenses as the Japanese were spending in Washington in the mid- and later 1980's—A large proportion of academic research by Western scholars who concentrate on Japan is funded by Japanese institutions.'" (*Marching Orders*, page 551.)

Professor Ronald Spector, Professor of History and International Relations at George Washington University's Elliot School of International Affairs, said that Gar Alperovitz had been pedaling his revisionist line for forty years. This "revisionist line" constantly proclaimed, "there is no consensus about whether the Bomb ended the War sooner or not. And there is no consensus on whether the invasion of Japan would have been necessary or not. And there is no consensus on what the casualties

For the information of all the Ph.D. professors—Harwit, Alperovitz, Kuznick, Lif-ton, Bernstein, and Neufield, et al.—who have tried to degrade President Truman's wisdom, sagacity and good judgment in the atomic bomb decision: Harry Truman had a Master's Degree in Human Experience and a Ph.D. in Common Sense. Harry Truman was a hero. Until the day he died, he had a clear conscience about the atom bomb.

may have been on the invasion of Japan." Winston Churchill placed the predicted casualties in an invasion of Japan at 1,200,000 with Americans being 1,000,000 of these. (Note: General Davis estimates 1,000,000 to 2,000,000 previously cited.)

The only reason that some mindless writer can assert that there is no consensus on these topics is that Alperovitz, Lifton and Mitchell, Kuznick, Bernstein, Harwit all have written long, and spoken loud, about the Bomb so as to create the impression that there is no consensus on any of the facts surrounding the use of the atomic bomb. The old adage "if you repeat something long enough and loud enough, people will believe it" is too true.

Opposed to that shallow unreasonable line of thought, and as a matter of fact, among all those who have any desire to know the truth, and who knew the facts at the time President Harry Truman ordered the dropping of the Bomb, there is really unanimity and a total consensus about the valid and proper use of the atomic bomb.

Winston Churchill asserted about the decision to drop the Bomb, "to avert a *vast indefinite butchery*, to bring the war to an end, to give peace to the world, to lay healing hands upon its tortured peoples by a manifestation of overwhelming power at the cost of a few explosions seemed, after all our toils and perils, a miracle of deliverance." The statement of this great British Statesman, added to all of the other facts surrounding the Bomb, should help determine for all time that the use of the Bomb was proper.

The criticism of President Truman by the revisionists named in this book, unfairly portrays him as not having the "extraordinary wisdom" needed to make the atom bomb decision. (Events before and after the atomic bombs were used, proved Truman *did* have the superlative wisdom and courage needed in making this momentous decision.)

Lifton and Mitchell in their book *Hiroshima in America* insultingly say Truman was "a tragic figure unable and unwilling to recognize, to touch emotionally, either his own tragedy or the human tragedy of the atomic bombings" — "His decision was prefigured but not foreclosed. In the end he decided to use atomic weapons on undefended cities because he was drawn to their power, and because he was afraid not to use them."

What Journalism! Undefended cities!! This was injected in the book to try to make President Truman seem heartless. Hiroshima and Nagasaki were as well defended as any Japanese city.

[Hiroshima was the headquarters of Field Marshall Shunroku Hata, who commanded the Second General Army. He is described in Professor Newman's manuscript (page 184) as a "fight to the end die-hard commander."

Gordon Thomas and Max Morgan Witt in *Enola Gay*, page 165-6, say that Hiroshima was "a beehive of war industry, hardly a home was not involved in manufacturing parts for Kamikaze planes and boats, for bombs, shell casings, rifles and handguns.]

Compare the bizarre claims of the revisionists with what actually happened.

President Truman appointed an Interim Committee to study and recommend use of the atomic bomb.

This committee was composed of some of the more outstanding Americans of that time: Secretary of War Henry Stimson; Dr. James Corrant, Chairman, National Defense Research Committee and President of Harvard University; Dr. Varnevar Bush, Director, Office of Scientific Research and Development; Dr. Karl Compton, Chief, Office of Field Service, Office of Scientific Research and Development; Honorable William J. Clayton, Assistant Secretary of State; Honorable Ralph A. Bard, Under Secretary of Navy.

This all-civilian Interim Committee headed by Stimson, considered a proposal to demonstrate the atomic bomb to the Japanese. They determined that such a demonstration was totally impractical.

1. The bomb might not explode. A disastrous consequence.
2. After selection of a suitable island, the Japanese could move allied prisoners of war there.
3. Difficult to arrange for Japanese observers to be transported to the site.
4. Japanese could attempt to shoot down the B-29 carrying the bomb.
5. Any attempt at a demonstration would require willing Japanese participation and a level of U.S.-Japanese

communications that was inconceivable in wartime.

6. The Japanese could spend weeks or months debating the demonstration.

The Interim Committee recommended to the President that the bombs be used as soon as possible against a military industrial target in Japan, and without prior warning (see Central Intelligence Agency Monograph, *The Final Months of the War with Japan: Signals Intelligence, U.S. Invasion Planning, and the A-Bomb Decision*, by Douglas J. MacEachin.)

This C.I.A. monograph notes that the intimidating proportions of expected casualties and the view that the bomb was a way to end the war quickly was the driving force in the minds of the U.S. leadership, even before the much-larger-than-expected Japanese forces on Kyushu.

Suggestions by Robert J. Lifton, Mitchell et al, that President Truman's decision, "...was prefigured but not foreclosed, in the end he decided to use atomic weapons on undefended cities because he was drawn to their power and because he was afraid not to use them," are all completely repudiated by the fact that the Interim Committee was advised in its deliberations by a group of distinguished scientists: Robert J. Oppenheimer, Ernest O. Lawrence, Enrico Ferni, Arthur Compton and others.

Any claim that President Truman acted without the utmost reasoned deliberation and advice from the best minds in the world is a LIE.

It is misguided journalism to attempt to degrade one of the most momentous proper decision-makers in all of history. For the information of these two literary geniuses, Harry Truman had a Masters Degree in Human Experience, and a Ph.D. in Common Sense. Harry Truman was a Hero. Until the day he died, President Harry Truman had a clear conscience.

Chapter 11
Rape of Nanking

The atrocities in Nanking, that were barbarously visited upon men, women and children captured by the Japanese Imperial Army December 13, 1937 are the most well known of any six to eight week period of the Army's decades long "take all, kill all, burn all" military policy in China. The brutalities included stabbing, cutting open the abdomen, excavating the heart, decapitation, drowning, punching the eyes out. Thousands of civilians were buried or burned alive, used as targets for bayonet practice; children were thrown into the Yangtze River. Soldiers competed in "killing contests" and sent the number of murders back to newspapers in Japan to be published (shown in detail at end of this chapter).

The disarmed police of Nanking were marched outside the Hanxi Gate and slaughtered. December 23, 1937 – 1,000 elders, women, and children were driven to the sandbank and buried alive in a huge pit. Another occasion, six to seven thousand were driven to the sandbank, sprayed with kerosene and burned to death, as the Japanese soldiers laughed wildly at the horrifying screams of the victims.

The Nanking egg processing plant had tens of thousands refugees; when the Japanese discovered them, they were all killed. Several thousand wounded and sick POW's, elderly and young refugees were forced into the river by the Japanese, sprayed with kerosene, burning them to death.

Iris Chang, whose well researched book *Rape of Nanking* details all the atrocities in their chilling horror, gave a speech at the Rape of Nanking Redress Committee meeting in San Francisco, which is an excellent summary of the atrocities.

RAPE OF NANKING

Iris Chang's Speech for the Rape of Nanking Redress Committee
(Mock Tribunal, San Francisco City College, October 24, 2003)

It is a great honor and privilege to be standing before you
today. I want to thank all of you for coming here this afternoon
to learn about a very ugly part of World War II history that many
of you may be hearing about for the first time.

We all know about the horrors committed by Nazi Germany
during the Jewish Holocaust. And we all know about the bombing of Hiroshima and Nagasaki, and how its aftermath launched
a dangerous new nuclear age. These events have seared our col-
lective consciousness, and form the scar tissue that we now recognize as world history.

But unfortunately, as Americans, we are by and large bliss-
fully ignorant of the wounds left by the Japanese during the Pacific Holocaust of World War II, and by this I mean the atrocities
committed by the Japanese against the Chinese, the Southeast
Asians, the Koreans, the Filipinos, and even our own American
citizens.

I'm going to use the Rape of Nanking – the subject of my
second book – as just one example to illustrate what the Japanese
did in many of the regions they conquered.

About sixty-five years ago, on December 13, 1937, the Japanese Imperial Army invaded the city of Nanking, then capital of
China. Within weeks, the Japanese not only looted and burned
the defenseless city but also systematically raped, murdered and
tortured more than 300,000 Chinese civilians.

300,000 people might not seem like a huge number until [it
is] placed into the context of World War II history. More people
died in Nanking than from the atomic blasts of Hiroshima and
Nagasaki combined. In fact, the death toll of Nanking exceeds
the total civilian casualty count of several European countries
combined, for all of World War II. So in other words, if you add
up the World War II civilian casualties for three countries —
England, France and Belgium — for the entire war, that would

STILL be less than the number of people who died in Nanking — just one Chinese city — in a matter of six to eight weeks.

But numbers don't tell the full story. There was a degree of torture and suffering in Nanking that defies human comprehension. An American missionary who was there said it was hell on earth. Women were nailed to walls or impaled after being raped, or nailed to boards and run over by army tanks. Men were hanged by their tongues on iron hooks or buried waist deep in the soil so they could be torn apart by German shepherds. Even small children were not spared—babies were tossed in the air and bayoneted on the way down, or thrown into vats of boiling water. The orgy of violence was so brutal that even the Nazis in the city were shocked.

This was not, as some Japanese claim today, a massacre perpetrated in the heat of battle against Chinese guerilla fighters or "secret Chinese gangs," as one Japanese official put it. This was a cold, systematic massacre perpetrated against innocent Chinese civilians and unarmed POWs after the city had fallen to the Japanese, a massacre that came as a directive from some of the highest levels of Japanese power.

The military had issued a KILL ALL CAPTIVES order at the time. And the Japanese soldiers carried out this order, even though most of the Chinese POWs had thrown away their arms and surrendered and posed absolutely no threat to the Japanese.

In their zeal to find soldiers, the Japanese killed rickshaw pullers, police officers, laborers and other men whom they merely suspected were soldiers. During the first few days of the massacre, the Japanese machine-gunned tens of thousands of Chinese men, buried them alive, used them for bayonet practice or decapitation contests, or sprayed them with gasoline and set them on fire. Some of these executions were efficient but there were Chinese men who died under the most slow, sadistic, and excruciatingly painful circumstances—they skinned alive, crucified, pricked to death by needles and even cannibalized.

After killing most of the men in the city, the Japanese turned their attention on the women. The Rape of Nanking is, without a doubt, the worst mass rape in World War II history and probably the second worst mass rape in world history. They raped great-grandmothers over the age of eighty, children under the age of eight; they sliced open little girls who were not built for rape and even gang-raped pregnant women before tearing fetuses from their bellies.

Now, I won't burden you with any more of these gruesome details, but I must point out that the Japanese army officials in Nanking not only sanctioned the rape but encouraged it. There is plenty of evidence to show that Japanese officers told soldiers that it was perfectly acceptable to rape as long as they disposed of the evidence afterwards—which meant, of course, disposing of the rape victims themselves. The officers also joined the soldiers in the rape, and even one of the top commanders, Tani Hisao, single-handedly violated more than twenty women in the city.

All in all, the Japanese raped more than 20,000 women and girls in Nanking, and some estimate the figure could be as high as 80,000. But the full effects of the rape cannot be measured on a tally sheet of statistics. Can you imagine the agony of the woman who survived weeks of gang rape by Japanese soldiers, only to find herself pregnant afterward? Or of the woman who faced the choice of murdering her own child or rearing a half-Japanese child she could never love? No doubt many Chinese women could not make that choice. For months after the great Rape, a German diplomat noted that 'uncounted' numbers of women were taking their own lives by flinging themselves into the Yangtze River.

Ironically, the Rape of Nanking did more than destroy the lives of individual women in Nanking; it also resulted in the creation of a giant underground system of military prostitution, which trapped hundreds of thousands of other Asian women into sexual slavery to the Japanese army. It is believed that the Japanese rape of women in Nanking had caused such a public outcry amount Western nations that the Japanese government tried to control the libido of the army by starting their own pros-titution ring. And so an estimated 200,000 women—most of them Korean and many also from other Asian countries—were forced to serve in what the Japanese government called "facilities of sexual comfort" to stop troops from raping women in regions they controlled in China. The Japanese established their first comfort station between Nanking and Shanghai shortly after the Nanking Massacre, in 1938. Decades later, the Japanese tried to insist that these brothels were run by private entrepreneurs, not the wartime government, but a Japanese professor by the name of Dr. Yoshiaki Yoshima at Chuo University, discovered evidence in a government archives that the system was indeed authorized by officials of the Japanese High Command.

Now, many of these comfort women—some still teenagers or children when captured—were raped by 20 or 30 or as many as 50 men a night, every night, for years during the war. Untold numbers of these women (whom the Japanese called public toilets) took their own lives when they learned their destiny, and others died from disease or murder. The treatment of these comfort women is another untold horror that could fill volumes, even libraries, of atrocity books. Only one in four women would survive the experience. Some women were raped by red-hot-iron rods so that the Japanese would 'sterilize" them from VD. Some were hacked to small pieces or rolled over nail-studded boards when they protested their treatment, their remains given to other comfort women to eat as a warning to those who dared defy the Imperial Army.

I wish I could say that this was an unprecedented situation where a few soldiers ran amok—a situation that was never repeated by the Japanese elsewhere. But that would be a false statement. The Rape of Nanking was policy—and constituted just one small fraction of the totality of Japan's atrocities across Asia. The Japanese invasion of China killed an estimated nineteen million to thirty-five million Chinese people during eight years of war. Millions more died in neighboring countries, as the Japanese Imperial army slaughtered Filipinos, Southeast Asians, Asian Indians, British and American prisoners of war—some of them in the most gruesome and sadistic manner. In secret laboratories such as Unit 731 in Manchuria, Japanese doctors conducted medical atrocities on American and Chinese prisoners, such as vivisection without anesthesia.

One of the most frightening aspects about the Rape of Nanking and other crimes was how ordinary the murderers and rapists really were. It shows how easily typical, law-abiding men can be trained to become efficient killing machines.

During an intensely militaristic period—created by an economic depression in Japan, a period of political instability and a belief that these problems could be resolved through the conquest of Asia—the Japanese soldier was taught to believe, both as a schoolboy, and then during his military training, that the Chinese were subhuman, almost as if they were another species.

On the battle field, young Japanese men were ordered not to view the Chinese as human beings, but rather, in the words of a second lieutenant, as something of "less value than a dog or cat." To numb their hearts of any feeling of sympathy towards human pain, Japanese soldiers were also ordered to engage in killing exercises, such as bayoneting or beheading live prisoners of war, so even murder would be banal and routine.

In fact, Japanese military culture was so contemptuous of human life that even Japanese life was not exempt from this process of dehumanization. One former Japanese soldier said he was trained to believe that the Emperor was a force greater than God and that next to him, all human life was meaningless. This soldier believed that loyalty was heavy as a mountain and his own life light as a feather, and that the greatest honor for a Japanese soldier in war was to come home dead.

Let me tell you why I wrote *The Rape of Nanking*. When I was a child my parents told me that the Japanese had turned the city into a bloodbath during World War II, and that my own grandparents barely escaped the carnage. An avid reader, I searched my local library for books on the subject, but couldn't find anything. Only years later, as an adult, did I begin my search in earnest, after attending an exhibit sponsored by the Alliance for Preserving the History of World War II in Asia. The photographs were so shocking that I knew I had to write this book even if I had to self-publish it. And so I interviewed survivors in both the United States and China and combed archives for records, and I discovered that Nanking Massacre was indeed one of the worst atrocities of world history. It had been world news in 1937, but later forgotten.

You see, the Rape of Nanking is really the story of two rapes. The first rape happened sixty years ago. The second rape is ongoing and it is the rape of history and justice.

To this very day, the Japanese take no responsibility for these atrocities even though the wartime government gave the orders to commit them. There are politicians in Japan who have gone on the record to deny that any of these atrocities occurred at all. But there is no lack of evidence on the Nanking Massacre and of other Japanese atrocities of World War II. There are hundreds of survivors still alive in Nanking who can testify about the massacre there. And in the course of my research alone I found thousands of unpublished primary source documents on the Rape of Nanking—diaries, eyewitness reports, letters, government dispatches—that were generated contemporaneously with the event in four languages. The *New York Times,* the *Chicago Daily News,* the Associated Press, *Reader's Digest* and *Life* magazines all devoted considerable space to news coverage of the massacre, and newsreel footage of the horror still exists.

But to a shocking degree, the Japanese have escaped the moral and financial responsibility that their counterparts in Germany had to face over and over again. The Germans have paid the equivalent of $60 billion US dollars to their victims and they will continue to pay several more billion by the year 2005. The Japanese paid almost nothing—not one penny in reparations to the victims of Nanking. The Germans have made profuse apologies to their victims. But the Japanese, on the other hand, have yet to deliver one sincere apology to the survivors of the Nanking Massacre of their families. In fact, several Japanese officials have openly proclaimed that the massacre never occurred, or dismissed it as a minor incident much overblown. Even more disturbing is the discrepancy in public education on the event. Germans are required by law to teach the history of the Jewish Holocaust in their schools. But the Japanese, far from mandating the study of its World War II aggression, have openly impeded efforts of textbook authors to do so, and even censored details of the Nanking atrocities and other wartime crimes from their school textbooks!

What I find the most outrageous is the fact that the Japanese continue to worship their Class A war criminals in the Yasakuni Shrine in Tokyo. These criminals were men who carried the Japanese master-race militarism to the point where it resulted in Japanese soldiers seeing the lives and sensibilities of other races as having no greater consequence than the suffering of insects. The worship of these men is not only morally reprehensible but the source of enormous anguish to victims of the Japanese throughout Asia. It is behavior that would never be tolerated if its parallel were practiced in Europe. The Japanese worship of these criminals is considered by many to be the moral and political equivalent of moving statues of Hitler and his cronies into the biggest cathedral of Berlin and honoring them as GODS.

There are those who believe that this history is dangerous, even harmful to peace and reconciliation, because it dredges up stories that could open up old wounds and old conflicts.

But I believe it is even more dangerous to forget. Crimes against humanity must never be forgotten or denied—not at the peril of human civilization itself.

Japan cannot move forward as a nation until it educates its young about the truth, the whole truth and nothing but the truth about its wartime aggression—starting with Nanking. A country that refuses to disclose basic historical facts to its people-a country that rewrites history for its people—is a country that jeopardizes its very future as a democracy and dooms itself to repeating the mistakes of the past.

As history itself has shown, the amnesia following one atrocity can inspire another. It was the Turkish genocide of one and a half million Armenians—and international apathy for that genocide—that emboldened Adolf Hitler in 1939 to forge ahead with plans for the Final Solution, which ultimately exterminated six million Jews. In fact, denial and amnesia are considered to be part of the final stage of genocide—first the victims are killed, and then the memory of killing itself is killed.

If there is just one thing that you take home from my discussion here today, it is that we as human beings have a moral responsibility to force countries like Japan to face up to their crimes and to try to prevent atrocities like the Rape of Nanking from ever happening again. This is why this mock tribunal we are about to witness is so important. Thank you very much for your time.

Chapter 12
The Rape of Manila

W hile the Rape of Nanking is the most well known of the Japanese Imperial Army's killing rampages, readers should know of a similar rampage in Manila. Wanting details on these Philippine atrocities, I contacted my friend Raul Goco, Solicitor-General of the Republic of the Philippines.

His reply and material is worthy of a separate chapter as it verifies the extent of, and truth of, the Japanese Imperial Army's inhuman conduct in China. While the Manila rampage, at its height of intensity (February 3, 1945 to March 3, 1945), did not last as long as the two month intense slaughtering in Nanking, the vicious, inhuman, barbaric killings and destruction in Manila was the same indescribable depravity that permeated the entire Japanese Imperial Army.

If you look at the map of China, Southeast Asia, and the area conquered by the Japanese, knowing they were in China and Korea from 1931 to 1945 and all the rest of the Southeast Asia and South Pacific areas from December 1941 until August 1945, you will understand our estimate of the 30,000,000 people slaughtered by the Japanese in what we call a Super Holocaust.

Republic of the Philippines
Office of the Solicitor General
134 Amorsola St. Legaspi Village
Makati, Metro Manila, Philippines

28 May 1996

Hon. Dan Winn
Senior Judge
Superior Court of Georgia
735 North Marshall Street
Cedartown, GA 30125
FAX# (404) 749-2117

Dear Dan,

I received your letter dated April 1, 1996 requesting for information about Japanese atrocities committed here in the Philippines during the last world war.

Attached hereto are two articles taken from the *Philippines Free Press* magazine, No. 6 Vol. 86 issue of February 11, 1995, which give a comprehensive account of the destruction and liberation of Manila.

Hoping that these two articles can provide you with the reference/ data you need.

With my abiding best wishes.

Very truly yours,

RAUL I. GOCO
Solicitor General

Philippines Free Press, February 11, 1995

SACK OF MANILA

It was not the act of a crazed garrison, but the planned purpose of the Japanese High Command

This account of the wholesale destruction of Manila and its people is based on affidavits of victims and eyewitnesses of Japanese atrocities. Their testimony was collected by U.S. forces that liberated Manila. The affidavits were contained in a report made to the War Department by the Commander in Chief of the Southwest Pacific Area. For the sake of brevity, the actual wording of the original affidavits has been in most cases condensed, but the stark facts are exactly as related under oath. For security reasons, many of the persons making affidavits must remain unidentified.

MANILA has been destroyed. The once proud city of the Far East is dead. Its churches, convents, and universities are piles of rubble, bombed and burned beyond recognition. Its civilian population has been raped and burned, starved and murdered, its women mutilated, its babies bayoneted.

The order that brought this about came directly from Tokyo. Reliable evidence based on interrogation of prisoners of war, military personnel, Philippine officials and civilians, and Japanese documents reveal the staggering fact that the sack of Manila and its attendant horrors were not the act of a crazed garrison in a last-ditch, berserk defense, but the coldly planned purpose of the Japanese High Command.

In the first three weeks of February, 1945, commencing with the liberation of the Santo Tomas internment camp, the Japanese began to burn and destroy systematically the churches, convents and charitable institutions of Intramuros, the old "Walled City." They destroyed all of its most sacred and historic properties.

They reduced to a rubble heap the fine old Pontifical University of Santo Tomas, the greatest Catholic University in the Orient and the oldest under the American flag. Only the ruined walls are left of the Manila Cathedral, the most beautiful church in the Far East. The Archbishop's Palace, hospitals, convents, schools, libraries were bombed and burned. The cultural monuments that made of Intramuros a miniature Rome have been obliterated.

Outside of Intramuros the Japanese destroyed, with the same cold calculation, Spanish institutions belonging to the Sisters of Charity. In Looban Asylum, when the Japanese burned the convent, were more than a thousand refugees, mostly women and children. In Concordia College there were more than 2,000 refugees—babies, orphans and foundlings, sick people, and the insane who had been transferred from the Hospicio de San Jose. Did the Japanese give these helpless people a comparatively merciful death by shooting them? They did not waste their ammunition on these women and children, these sick and insane. They closed the doors with chains, surrounded the building with machine guns to prevent anyone from leaving the premises alive, and then set the building on fire.

On February 10, 1945, a squad of Japanese soldiers entered the Red Cross building and proceeded to shoot and bayonet everyone there including staff doctors, patients, babies, nurses and refugees. Nurses pleaded for the lives of mothers with newborn infants but all were bayoneted or shot. Then the attackers ransacked the building for food and supplies. Modesto Farolan, acting manager of the Philippine Red Cross, escaped. Under affidavit he has described the Japanese atrocities.

On February 12, a Japanese officer and 20 soldiers forced their way into La Salle College where 70 people were living, including 30 women and young girls, children, 15 brothers and a priest, and the adult men of four families. All the inmates were shot, attacked with sabers, or bayoneted. Many who did not die during the attack, bled to death. The attackers attempted to violate young girls while they were dying from bullet wounds and bayonet slashes. The chapel was set afire and only 10 of the victims survived. The Father Superior, who escaped, described the massacre under affidavit.

On February 23, 50 bodies were discovered in a 12 by 15 foot room in Fort Santiago. The bodies, riddled with bullets, the hands tied behind their backs, were shrunken and have the appearance of malnutrition and near-starvation. These bodies were piled in layers, several feet high. In another room were eight bodies in the same condition.

On the same day, 30 bodies were found in a small stone building

15 foot square. The bodies were all burned or scorched. A Filipino, who had been bayoneted by the Japanese but had survived and escaped, directed an American sergeant to the chamber of death. He was one of 58 tuberculosis patients who had been removed from a hospital and brought to the area. They were left without food or water. Whenever the patients asked for water or food they were bayoneted and thrown into the building of the dead.

On February 24, a heap of 250 to 300 bodies were found in a 15 by 18 foot dungeon, which was barred and closed by steel doors. The dungeon was with every indication these people had died of starvation. Positions of the bodies showed they had struggled desperately to escape. American officers who opened the doors attested the stench was like a blast.

Even though the Spanish flag was prominently displayed at the Spanish Consulate, the Japanese torched the building and more than 50 people were burned alive or killed with bayonets in the garden. The Casino Espanol and the library were burned. The house of the Auxilio Social and the Patronato Escobar Espanol were burned. It is estimated that 90 percent of the Spanish property in Manila was destroyed.

The provinces fared no better. On February 1, 1945, the Japanese dynamited the sugar central "El Real" in Calamba, belonging to the Dominican Order. In Calamba 5,000 men, women and children were killed and the town was completely destroyed by fire. Five priests, tied and about to be killed, were saved and related under affidavit their experience.

In Intramuros most of the Spanish priests and brothers were conducted by the military police to two shelters in front of the Cathedral. When they were penned in the shelters, the Japanese soldiers threw hand grenades among them, then covered the entrances to the shelters with gasoline drums and earth, burying them alive. Out of 13 Augustinian priests, only two were saved. Franciscan, Capuchin and Recollect priests were killed in the same way. Outside Intramuros 15 Paulist and three Capuchin priests were killed.

Dr. Walter K. Frankel, 55 years old, a surgeon, urologist, lecturer on history of medicine in the College of Medicio of the University of the Philippines and 19 others, including men, women and children, were herded into a room and surrounded by gasoline, saturated and set afire. Those who tried to escape were shot. Frankel, his sister, and one other person survived. Frankel's story, with signed affidavit, described the tortures.

On February 7, on the southeast corner of Juan Luna and Modones streets about 50 mutilated bodies were found scattered in the grass, on the pavement and in a ditch full of water. Approximately one-third were babies or young children and about one-third were women. Most of the bodies were found with hands tied behind their backs. On the same day the bodies of 115 men, women and children were found on the grounds of the Dy-Pac Lumber Co. near the railroad station. The Japanese had shot and bayoneted these people and pushed their bodies into the ditches. Many adults and some older children were tied, while very small children had been killed without having been tied. The children were from two to 10 years old. Some of the women were pregnant.

Enemy documents about the massacre include a diary entry recording the death of 1,000 civilians by burning, a battalion order giving instructions for the disposal of civilians by burning, and an order instructing that all people on the battlefield, with the exception of the Japanese, are to be killed.

At the camps residence on Taft Avenue, the bodies of 45 women were found, cruelly mutilated, with evidence of assault apparent. In this group were several children, all of whom had been bayoneted.

The individual atrocities, as told by the survivors, were countless and barbarous. Women were slashed with sabers, their breasts cut off, their genitals pierced with bayonets; children were cut and stabbed with sabers and bayonets. Men, trying to save their belongings from burning homes, were burned with flamethrowers and forced back into the burning buildings. Few escaped. An affidavit made by medical officer John H. Amnese lists such wounds as teen-aged girls with both nipples amputated and bayonet wounds in the chest and abdomen, a 10-year-old girl and a two-year-old boy with arms amputated, children under five suffering from severe burns and stab wounds. Further evidence of atrocities committed can be found in any of the civilian hospitals in the area.

SOME OF THE AFFIDAVITS

The LaSalle College Massacre
Brief of Statement by Father Superior
_____Fathers

———◆———

"I am a nurse 22 years old. On at lease two occasions I was an actual eyewitness at the killing of an estimated 75 to 100 civilians."
—Carolina Coruna

———◆———

On each occasion, Japanese firing squads composed of about 100 soldiers armed with automatic weapons lined up the civilians at the intersection of Victoria and General Solano streets and mowed them down with point-blank fire. Womenfolk of the victims who ran out to plead with the soldiers were killed in cold blood before they even reached the soldiers.

I was living within the Walled City with a family named Velez on Anda Street. One night a Japanese sentry came to our house. He called into the shelter where we were seeking cover, "Are there any men inside?" I can speak a little Japanese. I came to the doorway and told him, "There are only women and a two-month-old boy." "Keep the baby quiet," he ordered. As I turned he fired and I fell, shot in the legs and paralyzed from the hips down. I feigned death, with eyes open, watching the sentry. He entered the shelter and approached Mrs. Velez, who held the boy in her arms, trying to cover its mouth so it wouldn't cry out. The soldier advanced with fixed bayonet and thrust the blade into the child's head. Mrs. Velez screamed in anguish and the soldier fired in her face, killing her instantly. Then he shot and killed Mrs. Velez's sister. From that moment on I do not have a very clear recollection of the events that followed....

_____ was bayoneted and his body thrown in the death chamber. The survivor showed a bayonet wound in his back inflicted when he asked for water. The regimental surgeon inspected the scene, but because of the burned and seared condition of the bodies it was difficult to determine the manner of death. Wounds could be seen in the chest and stomach regions of some of the bodies.

Later a third group of bodies was found under circumstances that indicated a more diabolical, cruel and premeditated form of atrocity than evidenced by the others. A strong smell of decomposing flesh led to their discovery. Probing in the rubble of a dungeoned area disclosed two closed steel doors. These were opened with difficulty, and the stench struck the investigators with physical force. The dungeon walls were five-foot thick. The one high window was tightly sealed. Two feet behind the steel doors was a locked steel-bar door. Inside the airless 15-by-18-foot cage were other steel-bar separations. It is estimated that the room contained 250 to 300 bodies. It was impossible to detect wounds on the partly decomposed bodies, and there was every indication that they had died of starvation.

———

"An estimated 400 bodies were found in three different places in the Fort Santiago sector. Death from all appearances had been caused by shooting, bayoneting, or starvation." —Report of the 129th Infantry Regiment

———

The first group of dead consisted of approximately 50 bodies with hands tied behind them. The bodies were stacked in layers, face down, with from three to six bullet holes in each. Their position indicated that a row of victims had been faced against the wall and shot in the back. Then a second row was shot to fall over the first. Then a third and a fourth. The bodies were shrunken, giving evidence of near-starvation.

The second group of about 30 bodies was found in a stone building 15 feet square. When it was first discovered, the building could not be approached because of the heat of nearby fires. Later it was learned from a Filipino survivor that a group of 58 tubercular patients had been moved to this area from the hospital and left without food or water for two weeks. Whenever a civilian asked for water or food he was bayoneted and thrown into the building of the dead.

"I did not want to die by suffocation"—Father _____

The Spaniards were separated from the Filipinos and forced to enter the shelters in front of the Cathedral. In my shelter there must have been over 80 people, many of them priests like myself. In about half an hour the Japanese soldiers began throwing hand grenades through the air holes. We were all very badly wounded. We rushed to the door and the Japanese met us with a volley of fire and laughter. Then they covered the entrance with stones, gasoline barrels, and earth, burying us alive. That night, I dug a hole through the earth to breathe through. In the morning a Jap soldier saw the hole, fired several shots through it and packed the earth down again. After awhile I opened it again. I was lying on top of the decomposing corpses of my companions—there were already worms in them—and a swarm of flies covered everything. I managed to enlarge the hole enough for a companion and myself to escape at midnight of the fourth night.

One side of my body was covered with grenade wounds and my companion's wounds were worse. Rolling on the ground most of the way, torn by barbed wire and sharp rubble, we searched for water, food and shelter. We did not find food, but I found water in the tank of a toilet at the Bureau of Justice. The next morning I heard footsteps approaching my hiding place and a voice called "Come on. Come on out." It was an American soldier.

I believe we were the only ones to escape. Later I learned that the thousand or more Filipinos who were separated from us in the beginning had been covered with gasoline and burned alive....

"I, Modesto Farolan, age 45, Filipino citizen, witnessed the massacre in the Red Cross building on 10 February ."—Modesto Farolan, Acting Manager, Philippine Red Cross

The story of the Red Cross service to the people of besieged Manila is written in the blood of its own doctors and nurses who fell victims of Japanese bullets and bayonets at 6 o'clock on the evening of 10 February 1945, murdered in cold blood with their patients and the many refugees, mostly women and children, given shelter when their homes were burned or destroyed.

From Sunday, 4 February, to 10 February, my staff of doctors and nurses worked continuously day and night, without letup, hardly without sleep, food, etc., and without ever leaving the place, for since Tuesday the entire neighborhood was barricaded by the Japanese.

Suddenly, Saturday afternoon, a squad of Japanese soldiers entered the Red Cross building and began to shoot and bayonet everybody they found in the building. Dr. de Venecia, a voluntary surgeon, was preparing with an attendant two cases for operation. Miss Rosario Andaya, a nurse on volunteer duty was out at the main corridor keeping order among the large crowd that filled the building to overflowing. As we heard the noise of rifle fire in every section of the building, Miss Andaya screamed for mercy to spare the lives of a mother and child beside her. Before we knew what had happened, a soldier with drawn bayonet came into the temporary combined office-operating room-ward where I was and all of us, Dr. de Venecia who had just walked over to my corner, Misses Loveriza and de Paz, both nurses, and an attendant, ducked into our respective corners for safety. First, Dr. de Venecia was shot twice [as] he [sat] at his corner. The soldier next aimed at the attendant beside him but missed her but she threw herself over to where the two nurses had covered themselves with mattresses beside my desk and saw two patients crouching underneath. One bayonet thrust finished each of them. Another bayonet thrust at the girl that escaped the first shot, caught Miss de Paz underneath. Looking underneath my desk, the soldier fired two shots at me but the bullets passed between my feet, scraping the bottom rim of my Red Cross steel helmet. After me, he shot a young mother with her 10-day-old baby, along with her mother, the baby's grandmother, who was nursing the two. That, for all the Japanese knew, finished all of us in the room without exception.

More shootings went on around the rest of the building. From where we were we could hear victims in their death agony, the shrill cries of children and the sobs of dying mothers and girls....

The first Filipino scout of the advance columns of the American forces reach the Red Cross area at 7 in the morning of February 13 and warned everybody to clear the area for street fighting. I called to the few survivors to leave. As we began to run, the Japanese machine-gunned us indiscriminately. How many perished in the massacre, I cannot tell.

WAR AND REMEMBRANCE

Conclusion: As Dionisio fled he saw a Japanese soldier pick a baby up, throw it in the air, and catch it with a fixed bayonet.

By Nati Nugui

A paragraph in the resume of Manuel C. Colayco, who is being honored this month as the first casualty in the battle for the liberation of Manila from the Japanese occupation forces 50 years ago, reads:

"On February 3, 1945, Colayco (who had served in Bataan at the outbreak of the Pacific War in 1941 as a lieutenant, later promoted to captain) met the advance party of Company B, 44th Tank Battalion, then attached to the First Cavalry Division, US Army. Its mission: to liberate Malacanang and the civilian internees (Americans and other foreigners) being held by the Japanese [in the internment camp at the University of] Santo Tomas. Colayco's job was to guide the troops through the city [to avoid] the mined areas. At the gate of Santo Tomas, he was mortally wounded {in the explosion of} a grenade hurled by a Japanese sniper. On February 10, one week later, he died at the US Army Field Hospital No. 29."

Thus ended World War II for Colayco, who went through the Death March after the fall of Bataan, and after his release from the O'Donnell internment camp in Capas, joined the underground resistance.

The Battle for Manila would last a month and in its ferocity and cruelty 100,000 civilians would die at the hands of the Japanese. Their commander, Gen. Tomoyoki Yamashita, had ordered them: "Kill the people and burn the houses and buildings." In many cases, women were raped before being run through with bayonets. The Japanese were running out of bullets. It was cheaper with the bayonet.

North of the Pasig the casualties were not as high. On February 3 Carmen Arambulo (born Cuevas), an education student at the University of the Philippines when the war broke out, watched from the windows of the family residence on Isabel Street in Sampaloc as trucks loaded with Japanese soldiers thundered past. The word had gone around—from the Filipino drivers of the trucks—that the Japanese were in retreat. The trucks were bound for the highlands of Montalban.

When the last of the trucks passed, a deep quiet took over. But Carmen Arambulo was edgy. What next? Toward 5 that afternoon the family heard a noise that began like a steady, distant hum. Then it grew louder, getting nearer. The Americans! "[The Americans are coming!]."

A group of survivors has organized Memorate Manila '45, whose task is to collect as many accounts of Japanese atrocities in Manila during the month-long battle and store these items in a time capsule that will be opened sometime in the future.

"What happened in Manila," said Miguel Perez-Rubio (former President Corazon Aquino's protocol officer), whose family was wiped out during the battle, "has to be told and remembered. In Asia, we are not the only ones who suffered during the war. I was a kid when I heard about the rape of Nanjing. I was too young to understand and if it happened to us. But then it happened too far from us. It is important to give testimony so that we don't become a mere footnote in history. The future generations of Japanese should also know what their forebears did here, if only [to prevent it from happening again]."

Perez-Rubio survived because he was a prisoner in Baguio of the Kempei Tai, the Japanese version of Nazi SS and Gestapo. Had he been in Manila, he would have met the same fate as that of his entire family. He was a guerrilla who had been ordered to go Baguio with another fighter in the resistance, Johnny Ysmael, son-in-law of Claro M. Recto, who was minister of foreign affairs in the Japanese Occupation government of Jose P. Laurel. Their mission was to help Manuel Roxas escape to the north and thence to Australia to rejoin MacArthur's forces. But the two were captured, sentenced to death, and only with the intermediation of Laurel was their sentence commuted to life. They were to "cool it off" until shortly after the liberation of Manila in the former Philippine Cold Storage in Burnham Park, which was converted by the Japanese into a prison. Perez-Rubio returned to Manila and heard from a family houseboy the gory story of his family:

At the family residence on Vilo Cuz Street in Malate, there was muted jubilation after reports that American soldiers had been spotted at Harrison Park, now Harrison Plaza. A houseboy, Jose, and Javier, a brother of Miguel, had seen the soldiers whose helmets were different from those of the Japanese. They thought these were American soldiers.

It was February 12, the same day 16 priests and civilians sheltering at the De la Salle College were massacred by the Japanese.

"Thinking that liberation was at hand, my father asked the family to take their dinner because they would probably be evacuated by the Americans very soon," Perez-Rubio said. "[But] instead of American soldiers coming, although they were really in the vicinity, it was members of the Japanese Imperial Marines who entered the house."

Everybody was ordered to go out and line up in single file. There were 15 to 35 of them in the house, including four children, the youngest six months old and another one year and a half. Besides the Perez family, there was the McMicking family, including Helen who was the fiancée of Carlos, oldest of the Perez-Rubio children. She was a sister of Col. Joseph McMicking, who lost his mother, two sisters—Helen and Consuelo—and a brother, Alfred, who served in Bataan.

"Alfred and a brother were beheaded," Perez-Rubio said. "The rest of the McMickings were either bayoneted or beheaded. There were also a few other people who had taken refuge in the house. A Japanese officer— who spoke quite good English—told them nobody was to talk. When [a youngster] did, [the officer shot him] at close range. The youngster died immediately. It was then that [the rest] realized they were all in danger. They were told to go back to the house.

"My family was placed in two downstairs bedrooms and the doors [were] shut [on them]. They heard furniture being moved around and [they thought] that these were being put against the doors to block escape."

The family did not realize that the Japanese were going to burn the house with the people inside. When they looked out the window, they saw that the Japanese were trying to make sure nobody had escaped.

"My sister Lupe, 17, with a group, was able to [get out]," Perez-Rubio said. "She [slipped out] through the front door facing Vito Cruz. I was given two versions of how she [was] killed. The first version was that she [was] bayoneted in the thigh and she bled to death. The other version was that she [was] first raped, then bayoneted. When I think about it now, [I prefer] the first version—to spare my feelings."

"Perez-Rubio's father, Carlos Sr., 58, brother Javier, 23, and houseboys Jose and Dionisio slipped out the burning house and fled toward Balagias

Street." "My father was shot in the head instantly. Javier was bayoneted in the back. Dionisio was able to scale a wall and [hide in] the cogon on Balagias Street. The next day the Americans came and saved him."

As Dionisio fled, Perez-Rubio said, he saw a Japanese soldier pick a baby up, throw it in the air, and catch it with fixed bayonet.

An aunt and an uncle stayed in the room saying the rosary. They were too old to escape. They died in the fire.

In one of the niches in front of the house, the bodies of six to eight persons were found the next day. One of them was that of Perez-Rubio's 58 year old mother. Another was that of his aunt Rosy, 52.

"The servants' quarters was also put to the torch," Perez-Rubio said, "and the servants were either shot or burned, among them Teria, my [nurse], whom I [considered] my second mother."

It used to be generally held that the Japanese were on a suicidal orgy, killing themselves after killing Filipino civilians as part of the ritual. A dead Filipino was one less to help the Americans when they returned. It was not known whether they went on a rampage individually or collectively, as a spontaneous urge, or on orders of their commanders. Later evidence was found pointing to the latter. They killed systematically. Some diaries were discovered and these contained instructions on how to kill the Filipinos—shooting them using as few bullets as possible or bayoneting them.

(Author's Note: The Manila and Nanking Massacres demonstrate that the Japanese Imperial Army's killing rampage was policy, approved by their leaders, and occurred over the entire China, Southeast Asia, and Pacific island areas occupied by the Japanese during the War in the Pacific.)

Chapter 13
Atrocities Unlimited

To more accurately understand the elements of why we must call the Japanese Imperial Army atrocities "Super Holocaust," we have to view a few of the pictures of their atrocities in China.

Most of these pictures were taken by the Japanese.

What could magnify the barbaric nature of these acts more than the desire by the Japanese to record them for the homeland to view, or as training material to condition their troops for more slaughtering?

Look at these hard-to-believe acts, depicted beginning on page 97.

****

JAPANESE ATROCITIES AGAINST
ZHEJIANG PROVINCE, CHINA

There were many incidents of atrocious retaliation by the Japanese against the Chinese in all the occupied parts of China for the most trivial of perceived resistance to the Japanese Imperial Army troops or the Japanese occupying authority. Any failure of Chinese to bow and show subservience to an Imperial Army soldier was reason for a beating or beheading. A particular retaliation atrocity we should note and remember is that against Zhejiang Providence in China.

Most Americans know of Jimmy Doolittle leading an air strike of sixteen planes on April 18, 1942, bombing Tokyo and four other Japanese cities. The planes flew from an aircraft carrier east of Japan. The aircraft carrier was discovered before getting close enough to Japan so that Doolittle's planes would have enough fuel to bomb their targets in Japan and fly to safety in China, beyond the territory in China occupied by the Japanese Imperial Army. The aircraft carrier had to turn away from Japan and proceed east out of range of Japanese bombers to save the aircraft carrier.

All Chinese (and Americans) should know of the aftermath of the Doolittle raid on Japan. Thirteen of Lt. Colonel Doolittle's planes had to crash into the sea or the fields of Zhejiang Province, China. The survivors were rescued and protected by Chinese in Zhejiang Province.

Japanese Emperor Hirohito immediately ordered retaliation on the Chinese in Zhejiang Province for these humanitarian acts. Japanese Imperial Army soldiers burned fishing boats along the coast, and where some American airmen had been rescued, the Japanese soldiers killed everyone in the village. Japanese soldiers used biological and chemical substances on the Chinese and an estimated 250,000 civilians were killed in this horrible retaliation.

The United States of America National Air and Space Museum in Washington, D.C. has a fine exhibit honoring the members of the Doolittle raid on Japan.

What should also be a part of this exhibit is a section honoring the Chinese in Zhejiang Province for their courage and for being subjected to the terrible revenge and slaughter imposed on them by the Japanese Imperial Army at the direction of Emperor Hirohito.

This is one of the only recovered "Kill All Prisoners" orders, which were in the hands of commanders of all POW camps. As noted in the main text, rescued prisoners from all Japanese POW camps stated that they were told by their guards that they would be killed when an invasion of Japan began.

Chinese POW used for bayonet practice as "live target" by Japanese soldiers, XyZhou, June 1928, near Nanking. (Politburo of Military Committee Taipei)

Bodies—murdered victims in Nanking, 1937. (Global Alliance)

A Japanese military officer beheading a POW. (Rape of Nanking, History in Photographs, page 144).

Japanese troops using live POWs for bayonet practice. (UPI/Betteman, Iris Chang)

A grinning Japanese officer chops off the head of an old Chinese farmer. (Global Alliance)

After a civilian was beheaded, his head was placed on display for all to see. (Global Alliance)

Japanese troops displayed the heads of their prisoners to demonstrate their "unchallen-egable authority" in China. (New China News Agency, Rape of Nanking, History in Photographs, Iris Chang)

Beheading a POW in Nanking, December 1937. (Revolutionary Documents, Taipei, Iris Chang)

Alliance for Preserving the Truth of Sino-Japanese War, PO Box 2066, Cupertino, CA 95015 (5-80)

A young Chinese boy selling candles was caught with 30 cents in his pocket. The money was issued by the retreating Chinese government. Possession of such currency in the occupied territory was considered a crime by the Japanese military. He was tied to a tree on 2nd Blvd. in Jinan, Shandong, and beheaded. (Global Alliance)

One of the 30 mass graves in the outskirts of Nanking, each with more than 10,000 corpses, resulted from the six weeks of killing in the city. (Global Alliance)

Chinese POW being used as a "live target" in bayonet practice, XyShou, near Nanking, June 1929. (Global Alliance)

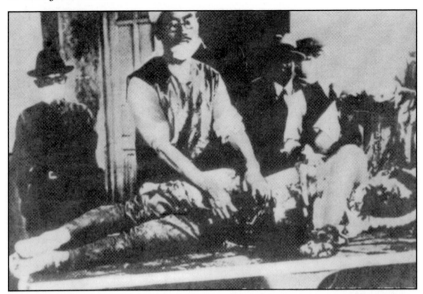

Japanese Army Unit #100, a biological warfare specialist performs a vivisection on a Chinese prisoner. (Global Alliance to Preserve History of WWII in Asia)

A Chinese woman disemboweled after being raped and killed. (Global Alliance)

A Japanese soldier stands over the bodies of Chinese POWs who were bayoneted or machine-gunned near Yuhuatai in Nanking. (Global Alliance)

Japanese troops used Chinese prisoners of war as targets for bayonet practice during the 1937–38 "Rape of Nanking". (Global Alliance)

"An Educational Special" for new Japanese recruits—the killing of POWs and civilians. (Rape of Nanking, History in Photographs, page 292).

This photo, stamped "Not permitted to release by the military, shows the brutal treatment of the Chinese POWs by the Japanese Army. (Rape of Nanking, History in Photographs, page 7)

These three Japanese soldiers wipe the blood off their mighty swords during a break from the killing contest. Said a reporter for the Tokyo Times, "I have never been to Hell, but there is a Hell, it was in this city." (Rape of Nanking, History in Photographs, page 140)

After the Japanese troops left Heng Yang City of Hunan Province in 1945, these dried bones and skeletons were discovered among several mass graves. The Chinese soldiers and civilians in the city had shared the same fate after the 47 days of siege of Heng Yang in 1938. (Rape of Nanking, History in Photographs, page 296).

Alliance for Preserving the Truth of Sino-Japanese War, PO Box 2066, Cupertino, CA 95015 (11-52)

A grinning Japanese officer beheading a civilian. (The Rape of Nanking, History in Pictures, page 131, furnished by Alliance for Preserving the Truth of Sino-Japanese War)

August 4, '95

Dear M/s. M. Nakagawa:

It' my pleasure that I found the right person to send these photos, because I always felt sorry for chinese people, and Japanese Imperial Army was so cruel unnecessarily, they were nothing but murderers. I found two pictures, very old. My descriptions about the pictures were not right, or I maybe have another one; I couldn't find it today.

Sincerely,
Setsuko Ikeda Tiffin
11736 Monte Vista Ave
Chino, CA. 91710

The family of a deceased WWII veteran of the Japanese Imperial Army sent this letter and two photographs to the Global Alliance from Chino, CA, after they had seen the photo exhibit of Japanese atrocities in Los Angeles, 1995. A Japanese American newspaper helped forward them to the alliance. (Global Alliance)

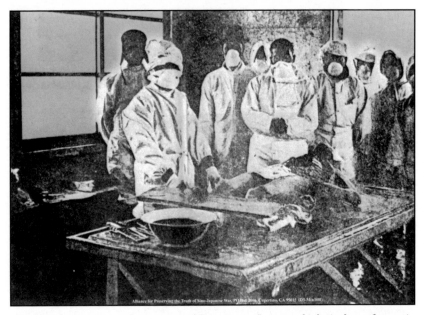

"Medical Specialists" of the notorious Unit 731, a Japanese biological warfare unit, watch their colleague perform an autopsy on a female victim and her baby. (Global Alliance)

Japanese troops slaughter a Chinese resistance fighter. (Rape of Nanking, History in Photographs, page 292).

The germ warfare factory set up by Japanese Army Unit #100 at MenJia Tuen, outside of Changchun in Manchuria. From the early 1930s through 1945, at least five different germ bombs containing contagious diseases were mass-produced each year.

A pile of bodies of children killed by Japanese troops, to be burned at LongWei Shan, TienLien or Iron Ridge—Dragon Tail Mountain at Liaoning Province, Oct.-Nov. 1931. (Global Alliance)

Victims of Japanese atrocities were usually the most vulnerable ones—women and children in Chinese cities and countrysides. (Alliance to Preserve History of Sino-Japanese War)

Chapter 14
Hell Ships

Hell ships were comparable in cruelty, depraved brutality, inhuman treatment and deadly torture to the other Japanese atrocities that stagger the mind.

Prisoners of war were thrown into the holds of these ships for their trip to Formosa, Shanghai or Japan for slave labor. Hundreds were crammed into the holds with no sanitary facilities, a minimal amount of rice and water (sometimes none) and with a bare hope of surviving, thus "hell on earth," until the ship reached its destination.

Ill: 1942. The *Tottori Maru* left the Phillippines on October 2 for Formosa, then the port of Pusan in Korea. That took thirty days, and Japan another twelve, finishing with more than a dozen dead bodies thrown overboard and hundreds of men off-loaded sick. The *Dai Nichi Maru* left Singapore on October 30; by November 11 men were starting to die, and by the time the ship reached Japan on November 25 there were approximately 80 dead.

Those deaths were from starvation, suffocation, and disease. Death in bulk quantity came from submarine attacks. In July, the *Montevideo Maru* out of Rabaul was sunk off Luzon by an American sub. It was carrying more than a thousand Australians—840 POWs, the rest civilians. None survived. On October 1, between Hong Kong and Japan, the *Lisbon Maru* was torpedoed, also by an American sub. Out of more than 1,800 British POWs, almost 850 were lost. (Prisoners of the Japanese P. 285 –by Gavan Daws)

Compare:

In January, 1942, the Wake marines and CPNAB contractors were in the hold of the *Nitta Maru*, a fast passage, less than two weeks Wake-Yokohama-Shanghai, no attack, and no deaths except the five men who had their heads chopped off.

Most other POW transports, though, were freighters—old, disreputable and cranky. The prisoners christened them the way they christened guards. *Hotsy Maru. Byoki Maru,* meaning sick. *Stinko Mar. Diarrhea Maru. Dysentery Maru. Benjo Maru,* meaning floating shithouse. (Prisoners of the Japanese, P. 285–by Gavan Daws)

The Japanese did not mark these ships as POW ships and most of the deaths (other than from suffocation, starvation and disease) were from the ships being sunk by the allies.

Oryoku Maru

By the end of 1944, the Japanese began moving able-bodied prisoners to Japan to be used as slave labor. If a man could stand, he was considered able-bodied.

Oryoku Maru left Manila on December 13, 1944, with 1620 prisoners of war (POWs), mostly American, packed in the holds. Japanese civilians & military personnel occupied the cabins. As it neared the naval base at Olongapo in Subic Bay, US Navy planes from the USS *Hornet* attacked the unmarked ship, causing it to sink on December 15. About 100 men died aboard the ship from suffocation or dehydration during the two nights aboard, while nearly 200 others were killed in the bombing or shot in the water as they tried to escape.

The survivors of the sinking were held for several days in an open tennis court at Olongapo Naval Base. While there, the prisoners were afforded no sanitary conditions whatsoever. Several deaths occurred and prisoners were treated like animals. The group of prisoners was then moved to San Fernando, Pampanga. While in San Fernando, 15 weak or wounded prisoners were loaded on a truck, believing they would be taken to Bilibid for treatment. It was revealed in the 1946 war crimes trial that they were taken to a nearby cemetery, beheaded, and dumped into a mass grave. Toshino and Wada supervised. The prisoners were then transported by train to San Fernando, La Union. There about 1000 of the survivors were loaded on another Japanese ship, the *Enoura Maru*, while the rest boarded the small *Brazil Maru*. Both ships reached Takao (Kaohsiung) harbor in Taiwan on New Year's Day, where the smaller group of prisoners was transferred from *Brazil Maru* to *Enoura Maru* and 37 British and Dutch were taken ashore. However, on January 9, the *Enoura Maru* was bombed and disabled while in harbor, killing about 350 men. The survivors were put aboard the *Brazil Maru*, which arrived in Moji, Japan on January 29, 1945. Only 550 of the 900+ who sailed from Taiwan were still alive. 150 more men died in Japan, Taiwan, and Korea in the coming months leaving only 403 survivors of the original 1620 to be liberated from camps in Kyushu, Korea, Manchuria, and Taiwan in August and September 1945.

Junsaburo Toshino, former Lieutenant and Guard Commandant aboard the "Hell Ship" was found guilty of murdering and supervising the murder of at least 16 men and sentenced to death as *Class B* war criminal at Yokohama. Shuske Wada, whose charges paralleled those of Toshino, was the official interpreter for the guard group. He was found guilty of causing the deaths of numerous American and Allied Prisoners of War by neglecting to transmit to his superiors' requests for adequate quarters, food, drinking water and medical attention. Wada was sentenced to life imprisonment at hard labor. All other guards received long prison sentences. The captain of the ship, Shun Kajiyama, was acquitted "as he had no chance to prevent any atrocities."

Junyo Maru

The *Jun'yo Maru* was a Japanese cargo ship (one of the "hell ships") that was sunk by the British submarine HMS *Tradewind*, resulting in the loss of over 5,000 lives.

The ship was built in 1913 by Robert Duncan Co. in Glasgow. It displaced 5,065 tons, was 405 ft. long, 53 ft (16m) wide, and 27.2 ft (8.3m) deep. The engines were rated at 475 hp (354 kW). In order to transport prisoners, it was fitted out with extra decks constructed of bamboo subdivided into cages of the same material. Deck space was also used for the prisoners.

When it was attacked and sunk on September 18, 2944, by the *Tradewind*, the *Junyo Maru* was packed with 1,377 Dutch, 64 British and Australian and eight American prisoners of war, along with 4,200 Japanese slave laborers bound for work on the railway line being built between Pakan Baru and Muaro in Sumatra. It was the world's greatest sea disaster at the time with 5,620 dead. Seven hundred twenty-three survivors were rescued, only to be put to work in conditions similar to those of the Burma railway, where death was commonplace.

[See Also Prisoners of the Japanese (P. 286)—Gavan Daws]

Chapter 15

Super Holocaust in China
(Japanese Atrocities in China, Korea, Southeast Asia and Against Prisoners of War in World War II)

J apanese atrocities, which I describe as a Super Holocaust, are far too extensive to be covered in one book; certainly not in a portion of this book.

But I will try to give you enough facts so you will understand why the Japanese have, since Prime Minister Shigemitsu, Minister Morishima (Lisbon), Minister Kase (Bern) and Minister Okamoto (Stockholm) in September 1945, initiated their propaganda campaign against the use of atomic bombs, tried to brand us as barbaric, and make the world disregard the horrid atrocities of the Japanese Imperial Army in the slaughter of humans and subhuman conduct never equaled in all of history.

From the time the Japanese invaded China, prior to 1931, and intensifying after September 18, 1931, they treated the Chinese as sub-human and tortured and killed them both systematically and randomly.

Unit 731, Unit Ei1644, and Unit 100—Japanese Army Units—were organized by authority of the Emperor, and designed for the purpose of developing, producing and experimenting with biological and chemical weapons of mass destruction. (*Factories of Death*, page 106.)

Unit 731, Unit 100, Unit Ei1644 produced cholera, bubonic plague, anthrax, typhoid, glanders, and experimented with snake poisons, blowfish poisons, cyanide and arsenic, and every conceivable disease.

They tested all of these on Chinese men, women, children, babies, and American Allied and Chinese prisoners of war. *Factories of Death,* by Professor Sheldon Harris, is a monumental account of the diabolical atrocities of Unit 731, Unit 100 and Unit Ei1644.

Professor Harris, a historian at California State University, says he cannot describe the atrocities of Unit 731 as they were "beyond science fiction."

Colonel Ishii Shiro formed Unit 731 (Unit 100, Unite Ei1644) in 1936 under mandate from Emperor Hirohito, and had more than 5,000 doctors, scientists and support personnel developing chemical and biological contaminants.

These units collected Chinese men, women and children, along with Allied Prisoners of War and Chinese prisoners. Prisoner victims were called maruta (logs) and were used as experimental guinea pigs in the most unthinkable inhuman tests ever.

Factories of Death (page 77) describes numerous diabolical, sadistic, deadly testing of pathogens on the Chinese in and around Harbin. In 1939 and 1940 more than 1,000 wells were contaminated with typhoid bacilli, devastating entire villages. Forty Chinese youth, thirteen to fifteen years old, in Harbin were provided lemonade with typhoid bacilli, contracting typhoid and dying. As an excuse to inoculate for cholera, innocent people in ChanChun were injected with cholera germs, creating a cholera epidemic. July 1942, Ishii brought 130 kilograms of paratyphoid "A" and anthrax germs, and an unknown quantity of typhoid to Nanking creating an epidemic to the delight of Ishii and his researchers. On this trip Ishii provided local children with chocolates filled with anthrax bacteria, with deadly results. Ishii provided dumplings injected with typhoid to 3,000 prisoners of war and released them to go home to spread the disease and die.

In July 1940 an actual biological attack, a five-month campaign of cholera, typhus and plague was spread through Mingbo (NR Hangchow) and five surrounding counties. Plague ravaged these communities for many years. Casualties were high.

With his immunity from war crimes prosecution secure, in November-December 1947, Ishii gave interviews on his work infecting human subjects with botulism, brucellosis, gas gangrene, glanders, influenza, meningococcus, plague, smallpox, tetanus and tularemia. (*Factories of Death*, page 65)

Many Japanese army workers in Ishii units later confessed to the horrible experiments on humans. Typical: "I committed a crime against humanity. I admit that testing the action of bacteriological weapons on living people by forcibly injecting them with serious infectious diseases, as was practiced by the detachment (Unit 731) with my participation, and also the wholesale slaughter of the experimentees with lethal bacteria are barbarous and criminal."

Testimony of Kauashina Kiyoski, Khabarousk Trial, page 58:

"The fellow knew that it was over for him, and so he didn't struggle," recalled the old former medical assistant of a Japanese Army unit in China in World War II. "But when I picked up the scalpel, that's when he began screaming. I cut him open from the chest to the stomach and he screamed terribly and his face was all twisted in agony. He made this unimaginable sound, he was screaming so horribly. But then he finally stopped."

The former medical assistant who insisted on anonymity, explained the reason for the vivisection. The Chinese prisoner had been deliberately infected with the plague as part of a research project—the full horror of which is only now emerging. After infecting him, the researchers decided to cut him open to see what the disease does to a man's inside. No anesthetic was used he said, out of concern that it might have an effect on the results.

The Japanese Army set up Headquarters of Unit 731 near Harbin, China to develop plague bombs for use in World War II. The research program was one of the great secrets of Japan during and after World War II, a vast project to develop weapons of biological warfare, including plague, anthrax, cholera and a dozen other pathogens. "The vivisection was also routinely used for practicing various kinds of surgery," says Dr. Ken Yuasa, a former Japanese doctor working in China during the War. "First an appendectomy, then an amputation of an arm and finally a tracheotomy." When they finished practicing, they killed the patient with an injection.

Medical researchers, with these units, also locked up diseased prisoners with healthy ones, to see how readily various ailments would spread.

The doctors put others inside a pressure chamber to see how much the body can withstand before the eyes pop from their sockets. To determine the treatment of frostbite, prisoners were taken outside in freezing weather and left with exposed arms, periodically drenched with water, until the frozen arm emitted a sound resembling that which a board gives when it is struck.

The doctors even experimented on a three-day-old baby, measuring the temperature with a needle stuck inside the infant's middle finger to keep it straight to prevent the baby's hand clenching into a fist. Victims were often taken to a proving ground called Anda, where they were tied to stakes and bombarded with test weapons to see how effective the new technologies were. Planes sprayed the zone with a plague culture or dropped bombs with plague-infected fleas to see how many people would die.

The Japanese Army regularly conducted "field tests." Planes dropped plague-infected fleas over Ningbo in eastern China and over Changde in north-central China. Japanese troops also dropped cholera and typhoid cultures in wells and ponds.

Professor Harris in *Factories of Death* devotes an entire chapter (15) titled "The Military and the Cover-up" to the "Faustian Bargain," in which the research was kept secret after the war in part because the U.S. granted immunity from war crimes prosecution to the Japanese doctors in exchange for their data. Beginning with MacArthur's headquarters recommendation that Ishii and others not be referred to the war crimes tribunal. (page 215)

Gregory Rodriguez, Jr. is quoted as condemning General Douglas MacArthur for promising General Ishii immunity from prosecution if he would surrender the records of Unit 731. "The lives of American FEPOWs (Far East Prisoners of War) experimented on by Unit 731 at Mukden were forfeited in the names of national security." (*Factories of Death*, page 118.) Gregory Rodriguez, Sr. was a POW at Mukden who had told his son of being a victim of Japanese BW experiments.

Frank James, a POW in Mukden from November 11, 1942 until his liberation in 1945, told of POWs being used as guinea pigs, and of his being assigned to assist in the burial of hundreds of those who had died from experiments. Frank James disclosed another unsavory shock when the U.S. Army required him to sign a statement that he would not disclose these atrocities, or be court-martialed. (*Factories of Death*, page 120.)

If these little atrocities are not mind-boggling enough, listen: "The U.S. Defense and State Department had a massive amount of material on the operation of Unit 731, having obtained them after the end of the war, through the immunity agreement with Ishii and others. Without going to the trouble of translating it, or preserving it historically for POWs who suffered there, it was returned to the Japanese government. Yes, the Japanese government. Continuing our complicity in helping the Japanese deny their atrocities so they can wail about our use of the atom bomb." (*Factories of Death*, page 122)

What happened to Unit 731, 100, Ei1644? Very predictably: See *Factories of Death*, page 99—"The Changchun BW factory and its satellite branches were destroyed by order of the Kwantung Army High Command during the closing days of the war. As with Ping Fan, all buildings were blown up with high explosives. Some expensive equipment, too heavy or cumbersome to transport, was also smashed. The rest of the equipment, and as much data and research material as could be salvaged, was transported back to Japan."

Unit 100 did not abandon Changchun until all prisoners were killed, those infected with pathogens as well as the healthy. No one was spared. Chinese workers at the camp were also eliminated. Prisoners and civilian employees alike were given injections of potassium cyanide. Only a handful of workers managed to survive the dosage given them.

A few lucky ones avoided the potassium ceremony, and lived to tell of some of their experiences."

Author's Note: Do you agree with Professor Harris that these Japanese atrocities are "beyond belief"?

While *Factories of Death* details some of the most diabolical and satanic experiments and killings by the Japanese, it is only a small volume of the slaughter by the Japanese Imperial Army which, I have already told you, was the most inhuman, savage, wanton, killing army in all of history.

Betrayal in High Places by James Mackay, a New Zealand author, is the best source for seeing the conduct of the entire Japanese Imperial Army as about four million savages on a rampage through China (1931 to 1942) exemplified by the Rape of Nanking, then from December 1941 until the dropping of the atomic bombs, rampaging through the Philippines, Hong Kong, Singapore, Indonesia, and all of the area shown by the map of their occupation.

Betrayal in High Places is about Captain James Gowing Godwin, a New Zealander who suffered as a prisoner of the Japanese, and as he learned Japanese fluently, he was assigned as a War Crimes Investigator from New Zealand and Australia at MacArthur's "Supreme Command Allied Powers" in Japan, after the Japanese surrender.

Godwin wrote, "…It was my determination to bring as many as possible of these cowardly bastards who beat up old men and women, to justice. I witnessed all the horrors of captivity, and endured them to a point [MISSING TEXT] and on many occasions, exhaustion. I was beaten and clubbed almost senseless many times over. I saw brave Allied servicemen beheaded and a very sick old man clubbed to death. At POW Camp 15D in Japan, I was almost starved to death and saw many fellow prisoners who simply died from forced labour, medical neglect and appalling malnutrition. To all those who suffered and perished I am resolved to do my best to atone their miseries and deaths, unlamented as seemingly they are. Fate has given me the opportunity to represent the victims of Japanese barbarity in a most privileged and sacred task. I will speak for all those who perished at the hands of the Japanese. I can do no less." (Dated 30 June 1947.) (*Betrayal in High Places*, page 101.)

Godwin verified countless slaughtering of POWs by the Japanese immediately prior to or following Japan's surrender.

August 15, 1945: "A couple of examples will suffice to confirm that in two instances alone close to 1,000 POW's lost their lives in savage acts of revenge carried out by the Japanese. I am defying a specific directive in revealing the following. Upon the orders of Field Marshal Hisaichi Terauchi and despite knowing that his Emperor had just made a surrender broadcast, Terauchi ordered the execution of 560 POWs in horrifying summary executions at Sandakan, North Borneo. The war criminals who carried out this massacre are still being caught. Hisaichi Terauchi

avoided the hangman by dying of alleged natural causes at Rengam, Johore Bahru, Malaya. The other murderous atrocity occurred at Aikawa
POW Camp on Sado Island where 387 Australian, American, British
and Dutch slave labour POWs were deliberately entombed at a depth of
400 feet in a worked-out mine which was collapsed by high explosives.
The date, 2 August 1945. There were no survivors. These premeditated
murders were nothing more than revenge executions." (P. 220)

Godwin's interrogation of Lt. Yoshiro Tsuda, second in command,
POW Camp 109 at Aikawa, Island of Sado, Japan.

Tsuda said on August 2, 1945, he was ordered to detail all of the 385
Allied POWs to the deepest part of the mine they were working, some
400 feet. The guards withdrew and the demolition of concealed explo-
sive charges were used to blow up the mine. Seeing the explosion Tsuda
stated:

"Knowing that the mine had collapsed in three separate places, I felt
certain all the prisoners were doomed. Upon returning to the camp I immediately reported to Major Sadakichi that the mine had been destroyed
and all 387 POWs entombed in its depths." (page 251)

Typical of the Japanese attempt to protect their war criminals, Tsuda
said all signs of occupancy of the POW Camp were destroyed and all of
the Aikawa guards and officers were given permission to return to their
homes. Imperial armed forces records sections (with the War Ministry's
knowledge) issued orders purporting to transfer all of Aikawa's military
personnel to the Kwantung Army. (page 252, *Betrayal in High Places*)

Interrogation of Saburo Yoshizaki revealed executions he observed
on February 9, 1942 at Laha Airfield, Ambon Island. Yoshizaki was a
civilian interpreter. Yoshizaki states:

He loaned his sword to the Japanese marine whereupon the latter
disappeared among a group of marines standing about hole 'B'. Yoshizaki
then described the execution of the first Australian prisoner at grave 'A';
this decapitation being carried out by Warrant Officer Kakutaro Sasaki.
He recalls that after the fourth prisoner had been beheaded by individual
marines keenly waiting their turn (ranks and names unknown) at grave
"a", several battery torches were procured to light the backs of the necks
of each successive victim. After the seventh or eighth Australian had
been decapitated at grave "a", the marine who had borrowed his sword

returned it to Yoshizaki commenting that it was blunt and the blade had unaccountably bent when he had beheaded a giant of a fellow.

Yoshizaki claims that he learned later that in addition to Dutch mortar personnel (about thirty prisoners), fifty-five Australian soldiers had also been beheaded on the night in question.

(2) concerning the second executions, Yoshizaki states that on his return to Ambon township on 23 February 1942 (he had been absent on interpreting duties at Paso) he heard from, he believes, 1st Class Petty Officer Tasuki Yamashita that between 15-20 February 1942 (exact date not recalled), all the remaining prisoners (Australian) at Laha Airfield had been decapitated, some eighty-odd as related to him by Yamashita. Yoshizaki avers that he told that this second execution at Laha had been carried out by crewmembers of a Japanese minesweeper that had been sunk previously by an enemy mine in Ambon Bay. It was an act of reprisal and retaliation for the loss of their ship. (P. 248, 249-Betrayal)

Godwin through his interrogations verified all of Professor Sheldon Harris' information on the horrors of the Ping Fan Biological and Germ Warfare Centre atrocities. (Unites 731, 100, Ei1644 (See P. 145-146-Betrayal.)

Godwin verifies the granting of immunity to members of these horrible units as described in *Factories of Death*. He and the other War Crimes Investigators were the recipients of the sickening directive from MacArthur's (SCAP) Headquarters. "The Ping Fan Biological and Germ Warfare experimental facility in Manchuria is to be neither discussed, investigated or entered into War Crimes Files." (P. 180)

With some verbatim, individual interrogations the reader can have some idea of the inhumanity permeating the entire Japanese Imperial Army. See the interrogation of Lt. Takeshi Sasaki:

GODWIN: Is courage and bravery part of the doctrine of Bushido?

SASAKI: Yes, it is fearlessness and bravery that derives from Bushido.

GODWIN: Do you think it is right to execute an un-armed civilian or prisoner?

SASAKI: If it assists a military objective, yes.

GODWIN: Can you define a military objective?

SASAKI: Yes, the pacification of conquered territory and disposal of prisoners.

GODWIN: Disposal of prisoners? What do you mean?

SASAKI: Either forced labour or their execution.

GODWIN: Do you comprehend the sanctity of life and the permanence of death?

SASKI: I consider dishonour more important than death. Death is a void, no more. To execute the enemy is to release them from the ignomity of defeat and the dishonour of surrender.

GODWIN: I find this contradictory. Japan surrendered and lives with the dishonour of defeat. Do you have double-standards?

SASAKI: The Emperor has asked that we endure the unendurable.

GODWIN: As a human being, and imbued with the spirit of Bushido, which would you value more highly, your own life or a hundred prisoners of war?

SASAKI: To obey an order is more important than my life or that of prisoners. I merely obey orders.

GODWIN: Who ordered you to execute the Australian prisoner?

SASAKI: It was my decision. I was troubled by the enemy taking up arms against the Emperor and the circumstances dictated the prisoner be disposed of.

GODWIN: What circumstances?

SASAKI: The prisoner had to be constantly guarded and it was I who was detailed to this useless task. Our patrol left our makeshift bivouac to go on a reconnaissance and search for enemy coast-watchers. The natives too, had to be taken into consideration. Some of them were armed and unfriendly.

GODWIN: Are you saying that you were left to guard the prisoner on your own?

SASAKI: Yes.

GODWIN: You didn't carry a sword. Where did you find one?

SASAKI: Our sergeant major left his at the bivouac. I borrowed it.

GODWIN: What was his name?

SASAKI: I can't remember.

GODWIN: Do you know that two natives witnessed you executing the prisoner?

SASAKI: It didn't concern me. Most of the natives were frightened of us.

GODWIN: Why did you chop off the prisoner's feet?

SASAKI: So he could not escape.

GODWIN: The testimony we have alleges that you securely bound the prisoner before forcing him to kneel. You then tied his legs together as well. Why?

SUSAKI: I was filled with a desire to punish the Caucasian and the enemy for starting the war. Japan at the time was winning glorious victories and I wanted to be part of this success in my own way.

GODWIN: You said previously that you wanted to prevent the prisoner escaping. Did you not realize that by severing his feet he would probably die?

SASAKI: He was going to anyhow. It was my intention to decapitate him.

GODWIN: Was there not an element of pain and suffering that you wanted to inflict first?

SASAKI: I prefer to call it punishment for taking up arms against the Emperor.

GODWIN: According to the natives' testimony, you waited for half-an-hour before executing the prisoner. Was this a deliberate delay to ensure maximum agony of the prisoner?

SASAKI: No. I had to wait because he lay on his side unconscious for twenty minutes. I wanted him in the kneeling position and alert to his fate.

GODWIN: Was this achieved?

SADAKI: Yes. He was barely conscious but managed to resume the kneeling position. I could tell by his pallor and the amount of blood on the ground that he had not long to live. I struck his neck once with the sword and beheaded him with one stroke.

GODWIN: Did you not consider your execution barbaric?

SASAKI: Japanese soldiers do not think such maudlin thoughts.

GODWIN: Now that the war is over, have you no remorse?

SASAKI: I did my duty as a soldier of Nippon.

GODWIN: You must realize that you will go on trial for this war crime?

SASAKI: I did my duty to the Emperor and my country. War is war. (*Betrayal...*, pages 174, 175 and 176.)

Colonel Masanobu Tsuji

Of all the evil Japanese, Godwin rates Tsuji, as the most evil of all. (page 124)

"Colonel Tsuji was attached to Japan's Department of Strategic Planning at the War Ministry. He was a man with a complete lack of conscience. Among the many war crimes attributable to him was the Alexandra Hospital massacre at Singapore, as well as the Singapore Chinese massacres.

"Following his posting to Manila where American and Filipino forces were collapsing under the sheer weight of numbers of Japanese troops, he was responsible for the following. Beleagured and surrounded in an exposed valley and woefully short of ammunition, three hundred American marines were on the verge of surrender when once more waves of Japanese troops hurled themselves onto precariously defended positions. But this was no ordinary attack. Colonel Tsuji, who was observing the unequal contest and well aware that the Americans must be getting desperately short of ammunition, gave an order that would seal their doom. "When the Americans surrender,' he said, 'take them prisoner then execute them."

"To the horror of concealed eye-witnesses–indigenous rural peasants who watched from vantage pints high in the surrounding hills—the surviving American marines who surrendered after their ammunition was exhausted were bound and formed in lines, all 280 of them, by their Japanese captors. Imploring with prayers and tears, the peasant womenfolk called upon their faith to stop the carnage that followed. Bayoneted, shot or beheaded, every prisoner was dead within two hours.

"It was Colonel Tsuji who ordered the Bataan Death March while expressing the wish that for any pretext, as many prisoners as possible should be killed. In furtherance of this notorious death-wish he announced, 'Japan is fighting a racial war and for the Emperor to triumph and to release our victorious soldiers to fight on other battle-fronts, prisoners must be executed.'" (page 122)

On one singularly bold occasion and following a desperate break-through on the Bataan Peninsula, close on 400 exhausted American sol-diers without supplies of any kind, including ammunition, were com-pelled to surrender to overwhelming numbers of the enemy. After being taken prisoner and under heavy guard, a platoon of Takasagto volunteers from Formosa was detailed to execute all the captured Americans. Such a large number of prisoners to suffer the death penalty must have pleased Colonel Tsuji who had arrived on scene. "Kill them all" he ordered, add-ing, "chop their heads off." There followed a most gory and bloody massa-cre of close on 400 white troops that is probably best left to one's shocked imagination. (page 124)

One more example of Tsuji's criminality should suffice. On 26 Sep-tember 1944, Lieutenant Benjamin A. Parker of the 14th Air Force, 25th Fighter Squadron, 51st Fighter Group flying mission F1027 and escort-ing Allied bombers, had his fighter aircraft hit by anti-aircraft fire. At the time Northern Burmese Japanese positions were being counter-attacked by Allied forces. Parker was noticed bailing out of his stricken aircraft by other pilots, but was neither seen or heard from again.

Parker was quickly captured by a Japanese patrol and force-marched to the area HQ of a Japanese forward command post. It was his unenvi-able fate that the officer in command was none other than Colonel Ma-sanobu Tsuji. There followed intensive interrogation with Tsuji playing a leading inquisitorial role. Despite dire threats and thuggery, Parker would only give his name, rank and serial number.

We have learned what followed from Japanese suspects being inter-rogated at Singapore. Enraged and with patience exhausted, Tsuji struck the defenceless airman with a slashing blow across the face with a steel bomb fragment. As blood welled from the deep wound he ordered Park-er's immediate beheading with a blunt Burmese sword. At the first blow Parker slumped forward, his head only partially severed. With blood well-ing from a deep neck wound his arms were gripped by watching Japanese soldiers before being raised back to his knees. It required two further strokes from the dull blade before his head was finally severed. Thereupon and at Tsuji's orders, Parker's body was DISMEMBERED AND THE FLESH TAKEN FOR COOKING AND EATING. (page 124) *[Au-thor's note: Further verifies cannibalism by the Japanese.]*

CANNIBALISM. Verified by Godwin, (also *Flyboys* by James Bradley and other authors)

War Crimes at Buka and Bougainville
FILE 125F CANNIBALISM BY 13TH REGIMENT IN 1944 AND 1945

(A) Interrogated Yukio Yoshida who denied he was a participant but admitted he was an eyewitness. He avers that the eating of human flesh developed into a COMMON PRACTICE and included the cooking of freshly killed soldiers brought back from the jungle. He was unable to say if the Australian bodies had been killed in action or intentionally executed.

(B) Interrogated Masuo Haraiwa who also had knowledge of cannibalism and who further admitted that army doctors would perform on-the-spot dissections of corpses. This entailed removing certain internal organs such as kidneys and livers. Occasionally a body would be rejected because it had been dead too long. Bodies that smelled or were fly-blown were left where they had fallen in battle.

(C) This testimony repudiates the assumption made in File 125E of the previous week's report regarding the belief that Australian soldiers killed in action were not cannibalized.

(D) Masuo Haraiwa's testimony also identifies that these atrocities were committed by members of the 2nd Battalion, 13th Regiment, near Jaba River and other places he cannot recall. (*Betrayal...*, pages 223, 224)

NUMA-NUMA

Executions of eight United States airmen and one padre at Numa-Numa in July 1943, have now been confirmed:

(A) Mitsuomi Yuda, formerly the Commanding Officer of 3rd Battalion, 45th Regiment, threw light on the above-mentioned atrocities. With his reluctant assistance, the where-abouts of the murdered men's graves has been located. All nine bodies were exhumed for possible identification before being reburied in a proper cemetery. The skulls of the victims showed sword damage and were found separated from the skeletons. Conclusively therefore, all the victims were decapitated. (*Betrayal...*, page 222)

FILE 158D DUTCH NEW GUINEA

It is now confirmed that decapitation of an Australian airman and flying nurse (Sister Craig) occurred at Babo in early September 1945. Though this was a remote area the world had been at peace for three weeks. (*Betrayal...*, page 224)

FILE 151G MASSACRE OF PRISONERS OF WAR, PARIT SULONG 1942

(1) Interrogated former Major Fukashi Hinokuma who had a grim story to tell and which was recounted to him in full detail over a meal by Staff Officer; Supply, Major Eisaku Morioka. It was Morioka who was detailed by the GOC to remain at Parit Sulong and supervise the mass execution. This is what was revealed.

The pretext used to entice the Indian and Australian prisoners to drag themselves to what was in effect, the designated execution site, was medical treatment, water and food. Concealed within the rear rooms of damaged shops, three squads of executioners waited behind tripod mounted heavy machine-guns. When all of the prisoners had arrived at the assembly point and were either sitting or laying prone, depending on the seriousness of their wounds, the machine-guns began their wicked thumping chatter of death. When cries of pain and shock were silenced, so were the machine-guns. Morioka mentioned to Hinokuma that seven prisoners had to be bayoneted despite the concentrated gunfire. They had still shown signs of life. Funeral pyres were quickly expedited per the simple method of collapsing six abandoned shops with mortars and hand grenades, following which 161 bodies were carried in an endless stream to the timber-dry debris and placed in piles where the engulfing flames would consume most efficiently. (page 240)

Lt. General Nishimura was sought by the Australian authorities for atrocities on Australian prisoners of war. The British at Singapore had sentenced him to a jail term and under the 'Faustian Bargain' (described by Godwin and Professor Sheldon Harris) Nishimura was to be repatriated, and sent back to Tokyo.

May 21, 1950, while the ship transporting him was temporarily in port at Hong Kong, Nishimura was transferred to the SS *Changte* on instructions of the Australian military authorities. From Hong Kong he was taken to Manus Island. In due course he faced trial in an Australian military court for ordering the massacre of Australian and Allied prisoners of war at Parit Sulong in Johore in January 1942. He was found guilty and hanged on 11 June 1951. [Judge Dan Winn's note: You gotta love the Aussies.]

James Mackay in his Appendix summarized the mind numbing scope of the quite incomplete *The Japanese Killing Fields* from the data Captain Godwin had secreted from SCAP Headquarters in Tokyo. He follows it with positive conclusive comments. (*Betrayal...*, pages 257, 258, 259)

World War II P.O.W.'S Thrown to Sharks by Japanese Gestapo

Hundreds of Dutch, American, Australian and British military on East Java in 1942 were 'punished' by their captors, the infamous Japanese Kempetai (the Military Police and equivalent of the German Gestapo), by encasing them in small bamboo pig baskets later to be thrown into the shark infested waters of the Java Sea. Details of this drama, one of the most grueling stories of cruelty against human beings, only recently surfaced more or less by accident after an 87-year-old Dutch veteran David Kriek demanded in July 1992 that the truth be known. File number 5284 in the General Government Archives' Netherlands East Indies section in The Hague, on inspection, proves to hold over 60 sworn eyewitness reports about the so called 'Pig Baskets Affair'.

THE JAPANESE KILLING FIELDS

COUNTRY	AREA	ATROCITY	VICTIMS	NUMBER	YEAR
Ambon Is.	Laha	Beheading	POWs	312	1942
Andaman Isles	Widespread	Massacre*	Civilians	1386	1945
Ballale Is.	Ballale	Massacre	Civilians	69	1942
Banga Is.	Serut	Beheading/Massacre	Civilians	103	1942
Batan Is.	Buyan	Beheading	Airmen	4	1944
Borneo	Balikpapan	Beheading	POWs	9	1942
Borneo	Banjarmasin	Massacre	Civilians	60	1942
Borneo	Loa Kulu	Massacre	Civilians	598	1945
Borneo	Pontianake	Shooting	Civilians	46	1942
Borneo	Sandakan	Massacre	POWs	560	1945
Burma	Widespread	Beheading/Shooting	POWs	138	1942-44
Burma	Kwai Railway	Slave labour	POWs	6960	1942-44
Celebes	Widespread	Massacre	Civilians	213	1942
Formosa	POW Camps	Starving/Shooting	POWs	170	1943-45
Japan	POW Camps	Sickness/Brutality	POWs	2315	1942-45
Java	Widespread	Massacre	Civilians	9800	1942-45
Malaya	Parit Sulong	Machine Gunning	POWs	157	1942
Maritime	Widespread	Massacre	Ships' Crews	1460	1942-44
Misool Is.	Binjap	Beheading	Airmen	5	1943
Moluccas Is.	Obi	Beheading	Airmen	3	1943
Neth East Indies	Maritime	Pig-basket Drowning	POWs	1390	1942-45
New Britain	Widespread	Beheading/Torture	Airmen	17	1943-44
New Guinea	Widespread	Beheading/Massacre	Mixed	640	1942-44
New Ireland	Widespread	Beheading	Airmen	17	1943-44
Palau Is.	Palau	Massacre	Civilians	37	1942-44
Philippines	Widespread	Massacre	POWs/Civilians	19740	1942-44
Sado Is.	Aikawa	Entombment	POWs	387	1945
Sarawak	Widespread	Massacre	Civilians	290	1942-45
Singapore	Widespread	Massacre	Civilians	13760	1942-45
Sumatra	Widespread	Massacre	POWs/Civilians	14000	1942-45
Sumba Is.	Widespread	Massacre	POWs/Civilians	144	1942-44
Sumbawa Is.	Widespread	Massacre	POWs/Civilians	291	1942-45
Tarawa Is.	Tarawa	Beheading	NZ Coast Watchers	23	1942
Truk Is.	Truk	Beheading	POWs/Merchant Navy	19	1942-44

*Massacre: Shooting, Bayoneting, Beheading.

COMMENT

As investigations are continuing to reveal more atrocities in the identified areas, the above totals should in no way be considered absolute. Further to, many areas collectively or individually, such as Banga Island, Dutch New Guinea and the Solomon Islands, as examples, have not yet fully discovered all atrocities committed by the Japanese. There were many instances of isolated executions particularly of Allied airmen that the Allied War Crimes Sections accept will never be solved. This difficulty also applies to deliberate massacres of torpedoed ships' crews where they vanished without trace, similar to the disposal of captured Allied personnel who were encased in bamboo pig-baskets by the Japanese, transported out to sea on coastal craft and heaved over-board to schools of sharks.

Atrocities perpetrated at sea and without evidence thereto, though known of, are difficult to prove at law without live eyewitnesses and sworn testimony. Fortunately, a few survivors from torpedoed Allied ships were able to confirm, despite previous Japanese denials, that their lifeboats had been rammed and machine-gunned, but they could not identify the Japanese warships or submarines involved. In the instance of wholesale pig-basket drownings and being torn apart by sharks, there were no survivors to tell of these sadistic atrocities. So far as can be determined, 1,390 POWs perished by this barbaric method of execution.

Finally, as intimated in the latter part of this chronicle, I have not attempted to correlate atrocities committed in the following areas. China, Hong Kong, Korea, Manchuria or Sakahlin. The task without proper documentation would be impossible, however, sufficient is known about the Rape of Nanking (1937) where 300,000 Chinese were massacred, and Harbin, Manchuria, where 60,000 prisoners lost their lives in biological and germ warfare experimentation, to realize that overall, the Imperial Armed Forces of Japan were responsible for the slaughter of hundreds of thousands of helpless victims wherever they rampaged.

In conclusion and to reinforce previous assessments, it would be no exaggeration to reiterate the appalling fact that so far as accountability is concerned, only one-tenth of Japanese wartime criminality, in an overall perspective has been uncovered. If, as present indicators suggest, investigations and prosecutions are wound down and cease altogether, then, for every ten atrocities committed by the Japanese, nine will escape punishment. The same parallel will apply (by deliberate default) to the lack of investigations into Imperial Japanese Army brothels. Approximately a quarter-of-a-million women and girls—some as young as thirteen—who were forced into sexual slavery, were denied justice by a man who, for political reasons, chose to keep the lid on a national scandal that would seriously embarrass his new Japanese collaborators. I refer to General Douglas MacArthur. (*Betrayal in High Places*, by James Mackay)

More Inhumanity!!

James Bradley in his book, *Flyboys*, documented the order for killing and cannibalism of a Navy pilot who had been captured along with his crew on the Island of Chichi Jima, March 9, 1945

Previous to this order, five other airmen downed at Chichi Jima had been executed and cannibalized. (pages 322, 323)

The sordid, inhuman beheading of Ensign Floyd Hall was even more beastly as he had been kept around the command post by the Japanese; Major Horie had begun to like him and they became friends.

Follow this 'sub-human' series of events: [page 284 et seq]

March 9, almost three weeks after Floyd was shot down, Major Matoba issued his order:

> I. The battalion wants to eat flesh of the American aviator, Lieutenant (Junior Grade) Hall.
> II. First Lieutenant Kanmuri will see to the rationing of this flesh.
> III. Cadet Sakabe (Medical Corps) will attend the execution and have the liver and gall bladder removed.
>
> Date: 9th March 1945
> Time: 9 A.M.
> Place: Mikazuki Hill Headquarters
> Battalion Commander: Major Matoba

Do readers think this is sub-human?

Chapter 16
Japanese Leadership: Suppressing the Truth

As history now stands, the world will always know the destructive power of the atomic bomb. We have never done anything to distort or diminish what occurred with the dropping of the bombs on Hiroshima and Nagasaki. However, unless we make sure at this point in time, that the world understands the use of the atomic bomb, *and its absolute correctness,* history will depict us as scoundrels.

Japanese writing and propaganda about the China War, Asian domination, Asian atrocities and World War II, and the atomic bomb, show that history is determined by the writer. It brings to mind a story about Winston Churchill. Upon disagreeing with a statement made by Prime Minister Stanley Baldwin, Winston Churchill declared emphatically, "History will say that the Right Honorable Gentlemen was wrong in this matter." After a brief pause he added, "I know it will, because I shall write the history."

The Japanese are saying what this history is, because so far, *they* have been writing it.

Every August 6 and August 9, we permit the Japanese leadership to focus the entire world's attention to the pitiful scenes as Hiroshima and Nagasaki. We are made to listen to the lamentations of those suffering survivors and bereaved families who have endured through prayer. We are made to watch the symbolic, sympathetic visit of Emperor Akihito to the monuments which have been erected to honor their dead. And then, like an actor on cue, Emperor Akihito delivers his lines to a world audience and speaks of his hope "that the world deepens its understanding of nuclear weapons." He claims to pray "for the repose of the victims and peace so that humanity will never experience such a disaster again." He speaks as if he is endowed with some logia-like omniscience.

The facts remain, the suffering at Hiroshima and Nagasaki was *minuscule* compared to the overall suffering caused by the Japanese military in China, Southeast Asia, Indonesia, The Philippines, Pacific Islands, Taihoku Prison and similar Prison Camps of the Japanese, the Bataan Death March, Bombing of Pearl Harbor, Hospitals in Singapore and also the *potential* 20,000,000 military and civilian deaths in an invasion of Japan.

Compared to this visit to Hiroshima and Nagasaki, it would be very nice if the Emperor would go to China and pray that never again will a Super Holocaust occur wherein 30,000,000 people are killed, and where a people are used like rats in experiments to prepare the military of Japan to be able to dominate the world; or at least to dominate all of China, Southeast Asia and the entire Pacific area. It would be nice for the Japanese not to continue to try to place a guilt complex on the United States of America for ending the war they started. It would also help future generations for the Japanese leadership to acknowledge specifically and not in only "pitiful generalized terms" their colonialism· and their atrocities.

Japanese leadership should specifically acknowledge (and document for posterity) the horrendous killings, and concentration camps all over China and Southeast Asia, document the activities of Unit 731, and the experiments on humans with anthrax, germs, plague and other biological weapons for military use. They should specifically acknowledge their "Rape of Nanking" and then we would really have something to tell the world that we hope never occurs again.

The United States of America joins with all who hope that the world will never have to experience the use of an atomic bomb again; nor experience a Pearl Harbor; nor a Bataan Death March; nor the killing of 40% of prisoners of war and people in concentration camps, nor the enslaving of millions of people of China and so many other small helpless countries; nor the dissecting of humans while they are still alive; nor the injecting of humans with plague and other killing germs to see how long it would take them to die. We hope that there will never be another military unit like the Japanese Military Unit 731 designed to use deadly experiments on humans as if they were vermin. We hope all of these things never occur again.

Emperor Akihito would do well to allow publications by the very few historians in Japan who are brave enough to want to give an accurate account of the Chinese invasion by Japanese military forces, and the aggression and horrendous, indescribable cruelty which occurred in China and through out Southeast Asia, and in the Pacific Islands. The Emperor and Japanese leaders would do well to allow these historians and the history books of the Japanese to reflect the true history prior to Pearl Harbor, and not to pass off Pearl Harbor as simply an occurrence which might, or might not, have happened. He should let Japanese history reflect that Pearl Harbor was the fault of the Japanese.

Again, I have never seen any official from Japan acknowledge that bombing our fleet in a sneak attack at Pearl Harbor, sinking a great portion of our Navy and killing thousands of Americans, was wrong.

The Emperor would do well to read Shelton H. Harris, a California State University Historian, *Factories of Death*. The Emperor would have done well to let the Japanese history Professor Saburo Ienaga publish his books on Japan's war crimes. He was stymied and ostracized because of his attempt to tell the truth about the Japanese atrocities and particularly Unit 731, the infamous unit conducting germ and biological experiments on thousands of humans in China. This professor's historical accounts have been censored and rejected by the education department in Japan and he was unable to publish anything. He took many years to try to publish his painful and true historic accounts. This great man died without ever getting Japan or its history books to say anything about the Japanese Imperial Army's atrocities before and during World War II.

No one has ever heard anything other than a vague, non-specific mumble that the Japanese regretted the war in the Pacific. No one has ever heard any statement that the atrocities in the Bataan Death March were wrong.

With this unbelievable propaganda campaign begun immediately after signing surrender documents, they have been almost able to obliterate from the eyes of the world their vicious military history. We must not let this continue to happen, *at our expense*.

Immediately after the end of the war, the Japanese decided they were the World Conscience on the Bomb, and on war, and peace. They first must have a conscience about their brutal unequaled, horrendous, military history before they start in on our conscience. As we say in the South, because the Bomb was dropped on them, it didn't "make their mouths into a prayer book."

Chapter 17
The Ten Most Awful Things That Should Never Happen Again

The pacifists, revisionists, "politically correct" and "distortionists of history" all have in their writings the theme, or hope, that the atomic bombings never occur again.

Using things we know occurred during and prior to World War II, let's put our perspective on a list of the "The Ten Most Awful Things" which all the world would hope should never happen again.

1. Japanese killing millions of people (30,000,000 Chinese, Southeast Asians, Pacific Islanders) while occupying their country.

2. Jewish Holocaust – 6,000,000 Jews massacred.

3. Killing of prisoners as part of an "Impending Defeat Plan," torturing and killing prisoners on a Bataan Type Death March, and torturing and killing all downed airmen, as occurred in Japan. (Japan, WWII)

4. Sneak attack on another unsuspecting country (such as Pearl Harbor, Japan, WWII).

5. Killing of civilians as a part of an "Impending Defeat Plan," as in the Philippines. (Japan, WWII)

6. Dissecting of humans as a military experiment, particularly while they are still alive. (Japan, Unit 731 in China, WWII)

7. Biological disease or germ warfare experiments on humans (Japan, WWII)

8. Bayonet practice on live humans, babies and children included, to toughen soldiers for killing. (Japan, WWII)

9. Teaching kamikaze practices; and that suicide, in the face of capture, is honorable. Teaching millions of civilians: men, women and children, that they must die for an emperor, who is God. (Japan, WWII)

10. Use of an atomic bomb (unless, of course, it is to save millions of lives).

Chapter 18
General
Douglas MacArthur

It is important that readers understand General MacArthur and his part as the Commander of the Armed Forces in the coming invasion of the main islands of Japan leading up to the dropping of the atomic bomb.

General MacArthur was an unusual military leader, in many respects a brilliant leader. MacArthur was the first in his class in 1903 at West Point. Only two others had a better record at West Point, one in 1884 and one in 1879 (that being Robert E. Lee the confederate General of the Civil War).

General MacArthur became Chief of Staff of the Army in 1930. He left that post in 1934 to become head of the Philippine Army as Field Marshall. He returned to U.S. service July 27, 1941 and was commanding General of the U.S. Army Forces in the Far East.

He had very positively expressed that he would be able to hold the Philippines against the Japanese in the event of an invasion. This proved quite wrong in 1942.

In a quite unusual occurrence in January, 1942, President Manuel Quezon of the Philippines gave MacArthur $500,000.00; a most unusual gift, which MacArthur should not have taken.

Another most unusual historical event, unknown by most historians, is that MacArthur supported Quezon in early 1942 when he thought about negotiating a separate peace with Japan.

This proposal outraged President Roosevelt who ordered MacArthur and Quezon out of the Philippines (*Codename Downfall*—page 46).

MacArthur's ego made him obsessed with the ambition to lead the invasion of Japan, which would be the greatest invasion ever, far surpassing the D-Day invasion of Normandy in Europe by the allied forces. This ego could have put the entire invasion force at risk.

In very early planning, MacArthur and the Joint War Plans Committee had estimated casualties for capturing Southern Kyushu at about 105,000.

The number of U.S. personnel for the Kyushu invasion at that time was 766,700. Instead of the 350,000 Japanese defending Kyushu, it later became known thru "Ultra" magic intercepts that the Japanese had about 600,000 defending Kyushu by August 1, 1945 (See *Ultra*, page 222, and also *Signals Intelligence Monograph*, Maps, pages 16 and 18). As the Joint Chiefs of Staff learned of the huge build-up of Japanese forces on Kyushu they became concerned about the success of the planned invasion of Kyushu and began to think of alternative invasion plans as opposed to the Kyushu "Olympic" plan, and asked for MacArthur's opinion on this. (See page 34, 35—*Signals Intelligence Monograph*)

After being asked by General Marshall about possible objectives at less defended sites MacArthur's dangerous ego and attitude was demonstrated as follows: He said he "did not, repeat not, credit the heavy strengths reported to you in Southern Kyushu."

MacArthur rejected any alternatives and dismissed the intelligence information as follows: "Throughout the Southwest Pacific area campaigns, as we have neared an operation, intelligence has invariably pointed to greatly increased enemy forces. Without exception, this intelligence has been found to be erroneous." (*Signals Intelligence*—page 35)

This statement of MacArthur was totally wrong. Rarely had his own intelligence and his guidance by "Ultra" receptions underestimated any enemy strength in the Southwest Pacific.

General Willoughby (MacArthur's Intelligence Officer) was, if anything, on the low side in any errors of intelligence (Signals Intelligence-P. 35).

Here was MacArthur willing to disregard his own Intelligence and the "Ultra" intercepts concerning the huge buildup of Japanese, but wanting to continue the invasion wherein his own Intelligence Officer, General Willoughby had begun to project the buildup being a (1) to (1) ratio of Japanese defenders to invasion forces and as he described "not a recipe for victory" (*Ultra*—page 222, 223).

This dangerous attitude by MacArthur was noticed by, not only the Joint Chiefs of Staff, but later recorded by all of the writers concerning MacArthur. To quote *Ultra*—page 223, "the notion of leading the greatest amphibious assault in history—14 divisions vs. 9 at Normandy—held overwhelming appeal to MacArthur's vanity. Fortunately the General was not allowed to test this egotistical ambition against the realities of Olympic, because the atomic bomb ended the war.

MacArthur's ego and dangerous attitude was also noted in *Codename Downfall* by Polmar, and also in *Signals Intelligence*—page 35.

This was not the first time MacArthur had wanted to disregard intelligence and pursue a campaign, which had dire predictions. When he had first returned to the South Pacific to lead American Forces, his first proposal (some said "demand") was to immediately invade Rabaul, New Britain Island. The number of U.S. and Australian troops and aircraft available to MacArthur at that time were not sufficient for an assault on Rabaul and his plan was totally rejected (See *Codename Downfall*—page 46, 47). More notably in history is MacArthur's removal as Commander of U.S. Forces in Korea in 1951 by President Harry Truman. MacArthur had challenged the administration's foreign policy and had proposed, during the height of conflict in Korea, to use Republic of China, Generalissimo Chiang Kai-Shek's troops to open a second front on mainland China and to send U.S. and South Korean troops above the Yaloo River.

President Truman and his Joint Chiefs of Staff were afraid that this could ignite World War III and because of this, President Truman relieved General MacArthur of all his commands.

In returning to the United States with his favorable wartime service he was a returning hero and treated as such in addressing a joint session of the U.S. Congress.

This also resulted in Truman being very low in his ratings with the U.S. public. There are many historical accounts of this, see: *Chronicle of the Twentieth Century*—page 98.

Later analysis of the Korean conflict verified that President Truman was correct, and to this day Truman's status has risen in the eyes of the U.S. public, whereas, as historians write more and more about MacArthur, his esteem has become lower and lower.

While MacArthur was never consulted about the use of the atomic bomb, it is also noteworthy that he was not even informed about the atomic bomb being completed and ready for use until July 29, 1945, when an instructional letter was sent to MacArthur and Admiral Nimitz concerning preparations for use of the atomic bomb. Nimitz however had known of the atomic bomb project since January 27, 1945.

Another insight into MacArthur's feelings about the Bomb appeared in an interview, after the Japanese had surrendered, by *Time* correspondent Theodore White. White noted that MacArthur was shocked when his air force had been destroyed on the ground at Clark Field, nine hours after Pearl Harbor, and lied to Washington about it.

Theodore White quotes MacArthur "whose blunders" White said had been buried beneath his victories, blamed the Bomb for ending the days of heroic military men like him. Not to even mention that the atom bomb could have saved millions of lives. MacArthur was quoted by White as saying that "scholars and scientists had stolen future wars from military professionals and made men like MacArthur obsolete."

He mourned that there would be no more wars of the kind that he knew. For this interview see *The Last Great Victory*, by Stanley Weintraub, page 436.

One must shudder at the thought of MacArthur prevailing upon the Joint Chiefs of Staff to pursue the Kyushu invasion (even in the face of intelligence indicating a (1) to (1) ratio of defenders to assault forces).

Would he have been as rebellious with the Joint Chiefs as he was later in Korea with Truman?

Undoubtedly, he would not have been that persuasive as the Joint Chiefs were well aware of MacArthur's ego and his tendencies to disregard intelligence information.

Betrayal in High Places, by James Mackay, describes how General MacArthur directed the war crimes investigators to not investigate some of the worst war crimes ever (Unit 731, etc.) and directed that these war crimes not even be discussed.

Beginning in 1945, some of these war criminals were given immunity, and other war crimes were ordered ignored by MacArthur. Beginning in 1949, many war crime prosecutions of the most heinous war criminals was stopped, and then all war crimes began to be terminated beginning in 1950, by MacArthur.

James Mackay, author of *Betrayal in High Places* serves up his feelings about MacArthur in his last comments in his book, "Approximately a quarter of a million girls, some as young as 13, forced into sexual slavery, will be denied justice by a man who, for political reasons, chooses to keep the lid on a national scandal that would seriously embarrass his Japanese collaborators. I refer to General Douglas MacArthur."

[We recommend *Betrayal in High Places* to everyone interested in the accurate recording of the worst atrocities of the Japanese, and the failure of our government to pursue the war crimes trials].

Chapter 19
Distorted History of World War II

The reader of this book must try to grasp the fact of the inhuman conduct of the Japanese Imperial Army in killing, torturing, raping, experimenting on humans (prisoners of war, women, children) with cholera, bubonic plague, anthrax, glanders, poisons; and being cannibals, yes cannibals (in eating the liver and meat from slaughtered prisoners of war). [See James Bradley's book, *Flyboys*—Death of Lt. Floyd Hall, page 284.] Also, *Betrayal in High Places*, by James Mackay, pages 184, 211, 223.

If you can grasp that, you will be challenged to make yourself believe that General MacArthur and his occupying military command acting for the United States, decided that the world should not know of these atrocities.

The image of Japan emerging on the world scene as a new "Imperial Democracy" (my designation) had to be SANITIZED. We could not have the "World" and U.S. citizens (first and foremost) knowing that the slaughter of Chinese, Koreans, Southeast Asians by the Japanese Imperial Army, vastly exceeded the 6,000,000 Jews killed by the Nazis in that Holocaust.

Prisoners of war and military personnel returning from the war against Japan were given military orders not to disclose Japanese atrocities, nor could they disclose torture to themselves. This distortion and obliteration of the inhumanity of the Japanese Imperial Army prior to 1931 through August 1945 has continued until today.

Peter Jennings in *The Century*, supposedly an accurate account of years 1900-2000, said much about World War II, 1941-1945 (Pacific Theater), but never mentioned the 19,000,000 to 35,000,000 killed by

Japanese nor any mention of Japanese atrocities listed here and described in the main text.

The *World Almanac*, which I obtained through *Reader's Digest* for decades, had this in all its editions:

WAR IN ASIA-PACIFIC

Atrocities. The war brought 20th Century cruelty to its peak. The Nazi regime systematically killed an estimated 5-6 million Jews, including some 3 million who died in death camps (e.g. Auschwitz). Gypsies, political opponents, sick and retarded people, and others deemed undesirable were also murdered by the Nazis, as were vast numbers of Slavs, especially leaders.

Civilian deaths. German bombs killed 70,000 British civilians. Some 100,000 Chinese civilians were killed by Japanese forces in the capture of Nanking. Severe retaliation by the Soviet army, E. European partisans, Free French, and others took a heavy toll. U.S. and British bombing of Germany killed hundreds of thousands, as did U.S. bombing of Japan (80,000-200,000 at Hiroshima alone). Some 45 million people lost their lives in the war.

Another History:

Chronicle of the 20th Century (1,374 pages), Chronicle Publications, Clifton Daniels, Editor in Chief. Quote: "the Book of our Century has finally been written." Distributed by Prentice Hall Trade, a division of Simon and Schuster, Inc. Has a number of sections about the Nazi Holocaust, nothing about atrocities or mass killings by the Japanese.

Cedartown High School, Cedartown, Georgia uses a history book *United States History in the Course of Human Events*, Historian Authors: Matthew Downey (Ph.D.), James Giese (Ph.D.), Fay Metcalf (Ph.D.).

This book has several pages about the Nazi (Jewish) Holocaust, in the killing of six million Jewish people by Hitler's German Nazis during World War II in Europe.

NO MENTION of atrocities, and killing of millions of Chinese and Southeast Asians by the Japanese Imperial Army before and during World War II in Asia and the Pacific (1931 to 1945).

Almost criminal, is the secretive hiding of the most extensive diabolical, inhuman (sub-human even) torture, maiming, slaughter, and cannibalism of human beings in China and Korea before December 1941 and then China, Korea, Southeast Asia, U.S. and Allied prisoners of war until September, 1945.

Quite predictably, even after Japan surrendered, many U.S. and Allied POWs were slaughtered by Japanese soldiers in final acts of revenge.

None of this in your typical encyclopedia, nor high school or college history book.

Where are all these historians who were so concerned about the atomic bomb and the *Enola Gay* exhibit fitting their distorted view of the end of the war; Alperovitz, Lifton, Kuznick, Sherwin, Mark Selden, Peter Jennings, Kai Bird, John H. Coatsworthy?

Coatsworthy—President of Harvard, President of the American Historical Association, at the time criticized the changing of the *Enola Gay* Exhibit and disparaged the "politicians, lobbying groups, editorial writers" and stated "why hire professional historians and curators to do an honest, thoughtful job, when you really want propaganda?" He was, without examining the issues in the flawed exhibit, stating that these people, proclaiming to be historians, should be allowed to exhibit the *Enola Gay* as they saw fit.

Where is Coatsworthy and the American Historical Association, when the entire World War II and decades of atrocities by the Japanese Imperial Army have been obliterated from history?

Where is Coatsworthy and the American Historical Association when Alperovitz et al. completely distorted facts about the atomic bomb to put their biased spin on history?

Immediately after the signing of the surrender documents by the Japanese on September 2, 1945, the foreign minister, Mamoru Shigemitsu began a worldwide propaganda campaign to brand the Americans as war criminals for using nuclear weapons. The goal of the propaganda was to keep Emperor Hirohito from being declared a War Criminal, and to divert western attention away from Japanese military atrocities committed during their China occupation prior to and during World War II, and their continued unthinkable atrocities against Allied prisoners. It was to divert world attention from their Super Holocaust (which exceeded the Nazi Holocaust) in Asia and the Pacific for decades prior to and during World War II.

An intercept of Japanese Military Communications showed that on September 15, 1945, Shigemitsu stated that since the Americans had been raising an uproar about the question of our mistreatment of prisoners, the Japanese should make every effort to exploit the atomic bomb question in their propaganda.

From that day until now the distortion of history has continued, and the Japanese have been able to totally spotlight the atomic bomb's use, as contrasted by Japan's Super Holocaust with its savage atrocities and killing of Chinese, Southeast Asians and Filipinos; and their horrible treatment, bayoneting and killing of our Americans on the Bataan Death March, and the bombing of Pearl Harbor, killing thousands of our Servicemen and civilians.

Bruce Lee in *Marching Orders*, pages 549, 550 and 551, gives a detailed account of how Foreign Minister Shigemitsu, with the help of Okamoto (Minister in Stockholm), Kase (Minister in Bern) and Morishima (Minister in Lisbon) promoted this devious propaganda campaign.

The group at the "proposed *Enola Gay* 1995 exhibit" at the National Air and Space Museum, Lifton, Mitchell, Kuznick, Bernstein, Kai Bird, and other revisionists are giving them support in that distortion, with false figures, anti-bomb slant, and really an anti-American philosophy.

Chapter 20
German Nazis vs. Japanese Imperial Army

The Japanese Military must be compared to the German Nazis. The German Nazis brutally killed 6,000,000 Jews in a vile attempt to exterminate that race of people. The Germans, under Hitler, proclaimed that they were a "Master Race" destined to rule the world. The Germans had a secret police force, The Gestapo, which could brutalize prisoners, civilians and anyone they chose, selectively. The Nazis and Gestapo of Germany are well documented in history. *Nothing can minimize the brutality of the Nazis, particularly to the Jews.*

Japanese Prison Camp Casualties = 100%

From about 1935 forward, beginning with the teachings of Colonel Hashimoto, the Greater Japan Young Men's Society taught the young men of Japan that they were a master race prepared for world domination. Just an example of routine practice for the Japanese Army was the murdering of 100 civilians on Wake Island, October 7, 1943.

As compared to the German Nazis, the entire Japanese Imperial Army was a killing and torture machine, treating all other people, including babies, children and women, as vermin or rodents to be bayoneted, to be dissected alive, to be cut open alive by scalpel, to be infected with plague or any disease for experimentation, to have their eyes punched out, to have their genitals cut off, to have their limbs cut off without anesthetic and while alive, and many other brutalities which might occur to a "Knight of Bushido." The Bushido Code authorized the Japanese soldier to do anything cruel, sadistic or deadly in the name of the military, or the Emperor. The Japanese had the Kempei Tai, which was the Japanese Gestapo. The Kempei Tai carried out all the above described torture activity routinely on all prisoners and civilians. Kempei Tai torturing and killings dwarfed anything ever attributable to the Gestapo.

Compared to the German Nazis and the Gestapo, the Japanese Imperial Army had Unit 731. Unit 731 was the most cruel and heinous of all Japanese Units, or of all Military Units ever. Unit 731 was the medical, biological, experimental unit which operated in China and specialized in incomprehensible dissecting of live humans to see how long it would take them to die from the loss of an organ or from an injection, or from plague, and to observe the results of deadly experiments before the unfortunate victim actually died. One of Unit 731's last acts after the surrender was to release plague infected rats near Harbin, China causing more than 30,000 deaths alone.

The routine torture or killing of prisoners by Germans did not occur. Some 3% of prisoners of war died in German prison camps, compared to almost 45% of Americans killed in Japanese prisoner of war camps. In addition to the unthinkable death toll in prison camps, 100% of the prisoners were subjected to the most inhuman starvation, torture, and humiliation ever conceived. Also torture and death awaited any who tried to escape, with the Japanese making an example of them in front of other prisoners, such as tying them to a stake and bayoneting them, or hanging them from a wire and beating them to death, any excuse to murder a prisoner. Not that it mattered to the Japanese, but all International Treaties prohibited punishment of a prisoner of war for trying to escape.

When we speak of prison camp statistics we list the percent of those who died in death camps and when we write about battles we talk of death and injuries and *total* casualties. It needs to be pointed out that in using deaths and those wounded as "casualties" the Allies had virtually 100% casualties in Japanese prison camps. No prisoners of the Japanese survived who did not have the equivalent of battle wounds. If it wasn't through bayoneting, beating injuries or torture, then it was through starvation. Yes, 100% casualties.

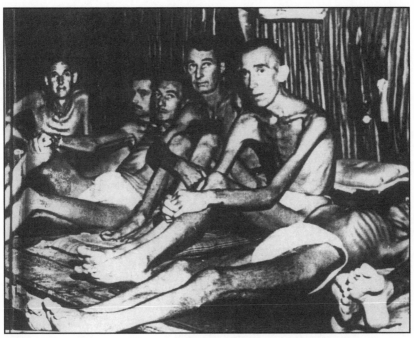

POWs from the infamous "Burma-Thailand Railway Camps" were walking skeletons at the time of their release in August 1945. Some 133 Americans perished building the "railroad of death." (Veterans of Foreign Wars Magazine, September 1995)

Chapter 21
Tenacity of the Japanese

If there was any question concerning the tenacity of the Japanese in their insane loyalty to the Emperor, it was certainly demonstrated after the surrender was proclaimed by the Emperor and the Japanese leaders. For many years after the official surrender on August 15, 1945, Japanese soldiers held out on many of the outposts of the Pacific War, even though on that particular island, or in that particular locale, they were living in isolation. The bushido, "way of the warrior" of the Japanese required them to fight the Emperor's war to the bitter end, and they demonstrated this for many years after the war had ended.

One, Sergeant Shoichi Yokio, held out for twenty-seven years after the war until 1972. He stated that, "Japanese soldiers were told to prefer death to the disgrace of getting captured alive." He stated, "I am living for the Emperor for the spirit of Japan."

Many holdouts stayed in Guam's jungles for many years and raided and killed natives and also military personnel on Guam. One of those Americans killed on December 14, 1945 was PFC William C. Patrick Bates, who was killed in an ambush by Japanese on Guam.

Even after this there were hundreds of Japanese still hiding in the jungles and remained a problem constantly until the last one previously referred to, Sergeant Shoichi Yokoi, surrendered. The battle in which PFC Bates was killed involved the Third Battalion of the Third Marines and involved a skirmish on the Asian-Piti Beaches and was some four months after the official surrender. Six Japanese were killed and about a dozen captured. Guam, of course, had dense, jungle-type vegetation and was ideal for enabling stragglers to survive for many years, and they did.

The most Japanese holdouts were naturally in the Philippines, the largest of the occupied islands, and between August 20 and October 23, 1945, 218 Japanese were killed and more than 67,000 were captured on

Northern Luzon. Then in November there were many more prisoners taken and one mass surrender netted seven hundred Japanese. As late as February 1946, the estimate of Japanese still in the hills and jungles of the Philippines was four thousand. It was estimated there were as many as eight hundred on Luzon, and six hundred in the Viscayan Islands.

The first Tarlac Regiment on Lubang Island near Manila Bay engaged about thirty Japanese, which had been terrorizing the area, on February 22, 1946. The US 86th Division accompanying the regiment reported at least six Japanese killed. On January 1, 1946, twenty Japanese stragglers wandered into the area of the 345th Graves Registration Company and surrendered. These seemed to be in excellent health.

One of the more unbelievable places in which the Japanese stragglers survived and carried on their undying fight for the Emperor was on the island of Peleliu. On April 21, 1947 about thirty-three Japanese soldiers came in after marine patrolling and surrendered their battle flag and sword to Navy Captain Leonard O. Fox. This group was lead by Japanese Lieutenant Ei Yamaguchi.

Peleliu had been captured and declared secure in October, 1944; and the main remaining Japanese garrison in the Palau Islands had surrendered September 2, 1945 but the diehards on Peleliu continued to survive until March of 1947. The renegade commander illustrated the leadership of the Japanese. He shot those who advocated surrender and demanded suicide for those wounded in encounters with Marine patrols.

The Marine garrison on Peleliu had been reinforced and Operation Capitulation was instituted to finalize the cleanup of Peleliu and as previously stated, the remainder finally surrendered to Captain Leonard Fox when Lieutenant Ei Yamaguchi turned over his samurai sword and battle flag and those under his command.

So the professors who arranged the failed *Enola Gay* exhibit, and those who wrote about how ready the Japanese were to surrender, should have carefully analyzed the Japanese indoctrination with their ancient code and ancient Bushido "way of the warrior, and worship of the Emperor."

Let me add one other important factor in the indisputable chain of facts, which show that Japan was not, and would not be, even thinking of surrender. Japanese recruits, home guard, and yes, civilians including children were training with packs of explosives, to throw themselves under tanks and blow themselves up. All ages of Japanese were formed into groups training with old firearms and bamboo spears. They were told that the Emperor expected them to resist to the death. Their motto: "One Hundred Million Die Together."

THE DECREE OF THE HOMELAND DECISIVE BATTLE
(Japanese War Ministry—April 20, 1945)

In the Regulations of Battle, the decree said that soldiers should be "the shield to our Emperor." They should be men "not afraid of death, believing the hope of reviving seven times to reward the nation, as well as delighting to become the foundation of the immortal Empire.

"During the decisive battle the sick and wounded shall not be evacuated to the rear" but would somehow keep on fighting and "annihilating the enemy force." There would be no retreat. Men were to stand and die. Other regulations ordered:

- Nursing and tending to comrades is not allowed.
- Units shall not retreat
- Every unit of the operational force should be a fighting unit. Even the rear, logistic, and medical units shall be prepared for fighting.
- Soldiers without weapons shall take the arms from dead enemy soldiers.
- Wounded soldiers and patients shall accompany troops during the march and participate in the decisive battle. Dropping out shall not be permitted.

As for civilians, according to the slogans that spread through Japan after the "Decree of the Homeland Decisive Battle" every man, woman and child was expected to fight to the death. People were told to sing a song entitled "One Hundred Million Souls for the Emperor." With the Decisive Battle would come "the Honorable Death of a Hundred Million, "who were also sometimes called "One Hundred Million Bullets of Fire."

Some zealots advocated involuntary sacrifices. In June, 1945, for example, a senior officer in Osaka said, "Due to the nationwide food shorting and the imminent invasion of the home islands, it will be necessary to kill all the infirm old people, the very young and the sick. We cannot allow Japan to perish because of them."

(*Codename Downfall*—Polmar & Allen, page 259)

Chapter 22
Yasukuni Shrine

The Yasukuni Shrine is a shrine at the northern edge of the Imperial Palace in Tokyo. The American people, in considering how the Japanese feel about history and the war, should know about the Yasukuni Shrine. This shrine is a national shrine. The Japanese built it to make heroes of all Japanese who fought for Japan and died in all their wars, including World War II. They are all considered kami, or gods, if they served in their military, fought for Japan and died, no matter how brutal or savage their conduct had been.

Yasukuni Shrine also includes all those who tortured and killed American service men in the Bataan Death March in the Philippines. It includes as Kami (god) all of the soldiers who brutalized and murdered the 300,000 Chinese in the 'Rape of Nanking' massacre. Also included as Kami, are all of the soldiers who rampaged across China and Asia and participated in killing the 30,000,000 Chinese during the occupation of a great portion of China and during World War II, in the most brutal of all military occupations.

It includes kamikaze pilots who killed American Navy personnel by diving planes into their ship whether it was a military ship or a hospital ship, and it therefore includes those who killed nurses with kamikaze attacks during World War II. A plaque to the Kamikaze pilots declared "the suicide operators, incomparable in their tragic bravery, struck terror in their foes and engulfed the entire country in tears of gratitude for their outstanding loyalty and selfless service." When I read or think about these emperor-loyal Kamikaze zealots dying for the Emperor, I always remember General George Patton's admonition to his troops; that in War, "It's not your mission to die for your country, but to make some other bastard die for his."

Further spitting in our face (figuratively) about World War II,

Japanese veterans stand outside this Japanese shrine and hand out bro-
chures stating that, "Japan's army in World War II fought in a noble effort
to free Asia from white colonialism."

The central hall of the Yasukuni museum contains such exhibits as
the forty-foot kai-ten human suicide torpedo and the ohka, or cherry
blossom plane, a light plane used for kamikaze attacks.

In short, any person who served in the military, no matter how brutal
they were, becomes a Kami, or god, upon death in combat.

Well, really one did not have to die in combat for the Emperor, to
be enshrined at Yasukuni. The most prominent War Criminal of Japan
who was executed, is enshrined there as a hero. Wartime Prime Minister
Hideki Tojo, and all the other war criminals who were convicted are enshrined there. We should mention here again, what a terrible job we did
in punishing war criminals in Japan, only a pitiful few.

The name of the shrine "Yasukuni" means "peaceful country." The
shrine is supposed to celebrate, "the soldiers who, since 1850 sacrificed
their lives so Japan could enjoy peace today."[3]

This Japanese shrine is an insult to the United States of America,
China, Korea, The Philippines, Singapore, Indonesia, and all the territories occupied by the Japanese (see Occupation Maps). This from the
Japanese government, which has criticism for our trying to put a historical exhibit concerning the *Enola Gay* in our Smithsonian Institute. How
dare they do this! How dare any 'wild mindless American support them
by distorting history in the proposed *Enola Gay* exhibit. All this while we
are trying, for some fifty years, to be delicate and understanding, and in
no manner wanting to offend the Japanese in the way we treat the Pacific
War, and allowing them to use the atomic bomb to place guilt on us and
make us the aggressors, and make the Japanese people the victims. This
has culminated in elaborate speeches condemning Americans as barbaric,
some sixty years after the war.

To the credit of the Japanese people, the best information available
indicates that a majority of the Japanese want the truth about the war
and the atrocities to be told, and do not support this misleading, flawed
shrine. It is a shame that the rabid self-proclaimed patriotic few, are able

---

[3]Many citizens of the United States of American and our Allies sacrificed their
lives so that Japan could enjoy peace today.

to be loud and dominant enough to prevail on this distorted historic theme.

Compare the vile insulting nature of the Yasukuni Shrine to our little pitiful attempt at a historic stamp.

In December 1944 the U.S. Postal Service was completing a set of ten commemorative stamps to mark the 50th Anniversary of the end of the war. The series was entitled "World War II-1945: Victory at Last" and the last stamp bore a picture of an atomic mushroom cloud and an inscription "Atomic bombs hasten war's end, August 1945." Totally historic. Totally correct. Well, what do you know! It offended the Japanese and gave them a chance to cry again about the Bomb. After they, a few of our idiots, and President Clinton objected to the 'insensitivity' of the stamp and the White House put pressure on the Postal Service to redo the design, the stamp was replaced by one with President Truman announcing the end of the war.

If you read this book and other valid accounts of the Japanese, you know that "*insensitive*" is a word Japanese should never dare to use to us, or the World.

Many blamed the Postal Service for being spineless, but the real gutless conduct was by President Clinton and the White House staff in not supporting the Postal Service, and saying that the Stamp was a fact we were within out historical right to proclaim. As a matter of fact it was not insensitive, it was fact. Follow their reasoning and we can't even celebrate the end of the war.

As a matter of fact, we cannot properly celebrate the end of the war. We're supposed to (in deference to Japanese feelings) call it V-P Day instead of V-J Day. (Author: 'We don't know who the hell else we were fighting in the Pacific')

Chapter 23

Early Surrender Theory (Professor Robert P. Newman Rebuts It)

All of the revisionists claim the Japanese were ready to surrender, and without their probing any of the facts or examining the post-war testimony, they based this on the conclusions of the United States Strategic Bombing Survey. Actually, they were the conclusions of one Paul Nitze, who controlled and wrote the final "Summary Report" and "Japan's Struggle to End the War," the major reports of the USSBS (and Nitze).

The most dogmatic statement, of what Professor Robert P. Newman calls "this counterfactual proposition" in "Summary Report" and "Japan's Struggle" was:

> *"based on a detailed investigation of all the facts, and supported by the testimony of the surviving Japanese leaders involved, it is the Survey's opinion that certainly prior to December 31, 1945, and in all probability prior to November 1, 1945, Japan would have surrendered even if the atomic bombs had not been dropped, even if Russia had not entered the war, and even if no invasion had been planned or contemplated."*

Gar Alperovitz, Peter Kuznick, Dr. Martin Harwit, the authors of the planned Smithsonian Air and Space Museum exhibit on the end of World War II, and all the other named revisionists swallowed this USSBS (Nitze) conclusion whole.

Professor Robert P. Newman (see bibliography) completely discredited this early surrender claim in a documented, well researched, well reasoned, well reviewed (by numerous scholars, see bibliography) manuscript written for Pacific Historical Review, 1995 by the Pacific Coast Branch, American Historical Association.

Professor Newman sent his complete manuscript on this subject to Brigadier General Paul Tibbets, Jr. (Pilot of the *Enola Gay*) who sent it to this author.

His manuscript title: "Ending the War with Japan; Paul Nitze's 'Early Surrender' Counterfactual."

Specifics of Professor Newman's Manuscript follow:

On September 9, 1944, President Franklin D. Roosevelt directed the establishment of a USSBS to measure as precisely as possible the effectiveness of strategic bombing in defeating Germany. Franklin D'Olier, president of the Prudential Insurance Company, was recruited to head the Survey; he was to have a civilian board of directors and extensive staff support from the military. The civilian directors included some whose later careers were prominent: George Ball, John Kenneth Galbraith, and Paul Nitze.

In June 1945, Nitze, Ball, and General Orvil A. Anderson, head of Air Force personnel working for the Survey, were brought from Europe to Washington, D.C. to advise on the most effective bombing plan for Japan.

While the USSBS was transferred to the Pacific to aid in planning air attacks on Japan, Nitze noted that "Fred Searles and I concluded that even without the atomic bomb, Japan was likely to surrender in a matter of months." "My own view was that Japan would capitulate by November 1945. However, the Joint Chiefs saw matters differently." [Author-- Readers will note that Nitze is an immediate expert on the war against Japan]

Nitze was in Japan from September 27 until December 4. For some of this time he had a thousand people working for him. In December, most Survey employees returned to Washington, D.C., where they processed their data and wrote reports. There were dozens of reports from various divisions of the Survey, but only three had the imprimatur of the chairman's office, (and hence of Nitze). Two of the three reports from the chairman's office claim that the atomic bombs had not been necessary to secure Japan's surrender. The most dogmatic statement of this counterfactual proposition appears in both the *Summary Report* and *Japan's Struggle:*

"Based on a detailed investigation of all the facts, and supported by the testimony of the surviving Japanese leaders involved, it is the Survey's opinion that certainly prior to December 31, 1945, and in all probability prior to November 1, 1945, Japan would have surrendered even if the atomic bombs had not been dropped, even if Russia had not entered the war, and even if no invasion had been planned or contemplated."

Here is a counterfactual proposition of breathtaking scope. Nitze obviously resented the fact that his ideas were not immediately accepted by the Joint Chiefs and Truman "and it was in the official reports from the chairman's office that Nitze was able to get back at the JCS, Truman, and their wrongheaded preference for invasion or nuclear weapons." (Newman Manuscript P. 171.)

As to the "all the facts" claim of Nitze, Professor Newman says, "It is absurd on the face of it to claim that a 'detailed investigation of all the facts' could have been made in a mere two months, especially in a culture alien to the investigators. But such elementary cautions did not inhibit Truman's critics. Gar Alperovitz, Hanson Baldwin, P.M.S. Blackett, Paul Boyer, Gregg Herken, Paul Keckskemeti, Robert Messer, Leon Sigal, the authors of a planned Smithsonian National Air and Space Museum exhibit on the end of World War II, and many others have swallowed this conclusion of the USSBS whole.

As to Nitze's theory that starvation would cause the Japanese to surrender: Plausible, this argument, but there are problems. How could the specificity of the dates of surrender be warranted? And how long would starvation take? Starvation as a cause of surrender is hard to evaluate. Hundreds of Japanese soldiers on isolated Pacific islands starved rather than surrender.

Herbert Passin, a member of the Occupation team "During the last year or so of the war, the Japanese military had stored away several years' supply of food, clothing, raw materials, equipment, and funds in its arsenals, caves, and other hiding places." Reliance on surrender by starvation is at best an iffy proposition here.

And both Nitze and revisionist writers assume that tightening the blockade around Japan until enough people starved to compel General Korechika Anami and his military diehards to surrender would have been a morally preferable way to end the war. Many ethicists doubt this conclusion. Whatever assumptions are made about the starvation level necessary in Japan's case (one million deaths? two million? ten million?), it is still true that starvation is a horrible way to die, and that the weaker individuals—infants, the elderly, the ill—bear the brunt of it. And the *official* position of the Japanese state was that a 'hundred million' would willingly die for the Emperor. The virtue of the starvation scenario must be argued, not assumed. Horrible as the 200,000 deaths from atomic bombs were, they do not automatically outweigh millions of deaths from starvation.

"Japan's Struggle" tells us how USSBS knows there would be early surrender: "The evidence is chiefly in the testimony obtained by survey interrogations."

Professor Newman takes the testimony of those Japanese officials who were interrogated and refutes, as follows:

1. Mikio Tatebayachin, Chief of the Civilian Defense Bureau, Ministry of Home Affairs. No help on "early surrender."
2. Matsuo Araki, Chief of Electrical Power Bureau, Ministry of Industry and Commerce. No help.
3. Admiral Tijiro Toyoda, former Navy Minister, former Foreign Minister, Minister of Mobilization, 1945. No help.
4. Etsusaburo Shiina, Japanese Total Mobilization Bureau, 1943. No help.
5. Genki Abe, Minister of Home Affairs, Suzuki Cabinet. No help.
6. Lieutenant General Masao Yoshizumi, Chief of Military Preparedness and Equipment Bureau. No help
7. Admiral and Ambassador Kichisaburo Nomura, Ambassador to U.S., 1941. Nomura believed that the people were willing to die fighting, that "it was the destiny of our country to continue this very unwise war to the very end." No help.
8. Prince Fumimaro Konoye, Premier of Japan, questioned three times. Former President of the Privy Council. He claimed that the

main obstacle to ending the war was opposition in the Army. He claimed that, even in July, 1945, had the Emperor tried to end the war, there would have been an uprising. Only in August was there a "decrease in the risk of disorders in the event of an Imperial rescript." And what factors contributed to the improved situation in August? Konoye did not hesitate: "The big thing was the deterioration of the war effort; then with the entry of Russia in the war, and the dropping of the atomic bomb, it did a lot to prepare the way for the next move."

Were this not plain enough, frame 0504 of the transcript has this exchange:

Q. How much longer do you think the war might have continued had the atom bomb not been dropped?

A. It is a little hard for me to figure that out.

Q. What would your best estimate be?

A. Probably it would have lasted all this year.

Q. It would not have been terminated prior to November 1-is that correct?

A. Probably would have lasted beyond that.

Q. Yet you said if it weren't for the Emperor's statement [surrender rescript] they would be fighting today, did you not?

A. Of course, that was a conditional statement. There was a limit to what they could do. They would do what they could.

Q. Hadn't they almost reached the limit?

A. Of course, they were nearing the limit, but the army would not admit it. They wouldn't admit they were near the end.

Q. Would they not have been forced to surrender, therefore, even if Russia had not come in or even though we had not dropped the atomic bomb?

A. The army had dug themselves caves in the mountains and their idea of fighting on was fighting from every little hole or rock in the mountains.

Konoye made clear that "The really big thing was to overcome the Army" to be able to end the war. Konoye refutes early surrender:

[Professor Newman points out that 'fear of assassination' was too great for any peace advocate to feel secure in promoting his beliefs. Every peace activist interviewed after the war mentioned this 'fear of assassination' should his beliefs become known].

9. Marquis Koichi Kido, Lord Keeper of the Privy Seal, Prime mover in the peace faction. Kido was close to the Emperor. Kido was the only Japanese to give any aid to Nitze in the "Early Surrender" theory. This without any factual foundation.

Professor Newman's account of how Nitze "badgered" Kido into Nitze's November 1 "early surrender" theory is very enlightening.

At first, Kido would not accommodate Nitze's position. The main obstacle to surrender was the army's determination to continue the fight, though Kido thought Minister of War Anami really wanted peace. And the Bomb? "The atomic bomb had a strong effect upon bringing those-for want of a better term I would use "fence sitters"-to the view that the war must be stopped. To answer the questions which of the two-the entry of Russia and the dropping of the atomic bombs-had the greatest effect on the army, I can not say."

There was more discussion of the role of the cabinet in the surrender and of the problem of securing army compliance. Then the interrogator went directly to his main point:

Q. (Probably Nitze)—In the event that atomic bombs had not been dropped and Russia had not entered the war, how long in your opinion might the war have continued?

A. As I have stated, our decision to seek a way out of this war was made in early June before any bomb had been dropped and Russia had not yet entered the war. It was already our decision.

Q. The dropping of the atomic bombs and the entry of Russia into the war apparently did speed the agreement of the services ministries to end the war. What we would like to get is the degree to which this was speeded up.

A. It was not the time factor. It was the fact that it made the task easier to bring the war to a close by silencing those who would advocate the continuation of the war. If there had been no dropping of the atomic bomb or entry of the Soviet Union into the war, I am inclined to be very doubtful whether the policy to bring the war to a close would have progressed as smoothly. A rather large-scale outbreak within the armed forces could easily be imagined.

Q. Is it proper then to interpret it as being your opinion that the war might have been over in any case prior to November 1st even without the entry of Russia and the dropping of the atomic bombs?

A. I personally think that the war would have ended prior to November 1, as every possible effort was being exhausted to terminate the war.

Here was the first, *and only*, affirmation by one of Japan's wartime leaders of the early surrender hypothesis. It took a bit of badgering and just a hint of suggestion; but Kido said it. He also said the effect of the atomic bombs was much greater than conventional bombing; Nitze did not want to hear that. But this was not the last word from Kido.

Kido said many things that were not included in USSBS's "all the facts." Arnold Brackman tabulates Kido's outpourings in *The Other Nuremberg:* 'his diaries contained 4,920 entries; his interrogations at Sugamo filled 775 pages… Kido's American counsel…put his client directly on the stand. Kido's week-long odyssey opened with his reading a 297-page deposition." Nowhere in all this testimony can one find even a hint at a belief in early surrender without the Bomb and Soviet entry.

And on the witness stand on October 16, 1947, at the Tokyo War Crimes Trial (International Military Tribunal for the Far East, or IMTFE), under questioning by an interrogator not possessed of USSBS biases, Kido made a statement contradicting what he had told the Survey. He identified the Nagasaki bomb as a "great shock to the nation, together with the Soviet Union's participation in the Pacific War… I thought there would be no course left but to broadcast an Imperial rescript to the nation… terminating the war" And free of USSBS badgering, he clearly indicated that he did not believe the war would have ended before invasion: 'It is my inward satisfaction that I was instrumental in saving another twenty million of my innocent compatriots from war ravages and also the Americans tens of thousands of casualties, which would have been caused had Japan gone on fighting to the bitter end…" if he kept Japan from fighting to the bitter end, he could not have believed in Nitze's early surrender hypothesis."

10. Admiral Soemu Toyoda, former Chief of Naval General Staff (member of the Big Six), Supreme War Guidance Council.

Toyoda had been one of the dissenters when Premier Suzuki tried to get agreement on a surrender in July [along with War Minister Anami and Army Chief of Staff Umezu).

Q. At what time during the course of the war would the Navy have accepted an Imperial rescript terminating the war?
A. That is very difficult to answer because even on the 15th (August) when the Imperial rescript to terminate the war was actually issued, even then we found it difficult to hold down the front-line forces who were all "raring to go," and it was very difficult to hold them back. I do not think it would be accurate to look upon use of the atomic bomb and the entry and participation of Soviet Russia into the war as a direct cause of termination of the war, but I think that those two factors did enable us to bring the war to a termination without creating too great chaos in Japan.

Toyoda's position on the morale of the Japanese people under bombing was no help to the early surrender hypothesis. He told USSBS that, "The effect on the people's morale was not as great as we had feared.... There was no idea that we must give up the war to avoid even a single additional day of bombing." General Anderson pressed him further on this; the Air Force wanted to prove conventional bombing had done the most to bring Japan to her knees. Toyoda did not budge. He admitted that "if the air raids were to continue for months... it would be impossible for us to continue the war," but he had voted to continue the war in August.

These were the interrogation sessions that might have provided Nitze with *first-hand* testimony supporting the early surrender hypothesis. Unfortunately, it is not here, except for the one constrained statement by Kido.

USSBS interviewed a dozen other high-ranking Japanese; their testimony was overwhelmingly to the effect that Japan would not have surrendered before the Bomb. None of them claimed the war would have come to an early end.

Professor Newman points to much other relevant testimony that Nitze had in his files but did not factor into his conclusion.

Lieutenant General Saburo Endo, chief of the Cabinet Bureau of Research, was interrogated. Endo was a soldier's soldier, and delighted in emphasizing Japanese fighting spirit to the seven Americans present. The Japanese, he said, were fighting for a righteous cause, and "winning" was not the big thing. After noting that neither Napoleon nor Hitler had won their wars, he said: "Whether we win the war or lose the war was not the primary purpose. Therefore, I told my men that they could fight without worrying whether they would actually win the war.... They should be willing to die gladly, knowing that it was unavoidable and that they were doing the right thing." Endo gave no specific statement on when Japan would have surrendered, but gave abundant evidence of the Masada attitude.

Atsuyasu Funada, Secretary of the Board of Information and former Foreign Office official. According to Funada, the Suzuki Cabinet wanted to surrender, but "the die-hards among the military still held out. The hopes of the die-hards were dashed to pieces by participation in the war by Russia and the atomic bomb. Both of these gave good material to the peace group."

Field Marshal Shunroku Hata, Commanding General of the 2nd General Army (Hiroshima) in 1945, was interrogated. Here was another bitter-ender. He stressed to his troops that Japan would win the final decisive battle of the homeland. The army would dig in deeply to survive preliminary bombing: "We intended to stand and fight on the beaches.... However, when the atom bomb was dropped on Hiroshima, I believed there is nothing more we can do, we might as well give up."

Baron Kiichiro Hiranuma, President of Privy Council, had been wounded by an assassin in 1941, and was one of the most important of the elder statesmen who engineered the surrender. Hiranuma claimed to be one of several Japanese leaders who advocated immediate acceptance of the Potsdam Proclamation. As to causes of surrender, "The biggest factor...there came the atomic bomb, so that the country was faced with terrible destructive powers and Japan's ability to wage war was really at an end."

On November 2, USSBS interrogated Lieutenant General Torashiro Kawabe, Deputy Chief, Imperial General HQ, who had been director of kamikaze operations in the Philippine and Okinawa battles. A fire-breathing supporter of war to the death, Kawabe intended himself to fly a kamikaze mission when the invasion came. He believed his forces had effectively concealed sufficient kamikaze planes near easily repaired runways to evade and withstand any American bombardment: "We believed probably we would lose the war and we knew we could never win the war; but we never gave up the idea of continuing the fight, using whatever [kamikaze] planes we could manufacture, and we intended to continue to fight unto the very end and make a showdown fight of it."

Fleet Admiral Osami Nagano, who had been Chief of Naval General Staff at the time of the Pearl Harbor attack, and was Supreme Naval Advisor to the Emperor at the end of the war.

Q. Admiral, could the war have been brought to a close, in your opinion, without the entry of Russia into the war and without the employment of either atom bomb?" Nagano acknowledged that even without these two events, Japan could not win, but, "Speaking very frankly, I think we would have been able to extend the war for a considerable time at considerable sacrifice on your part."

The Chief Cabinet Secretary at the time of surrender was Hisatsume Sakomizu, one of the peace activists; his interrogation on December 11 is one of the most interesting in the whole USSBS series. David B. Truman was in charge, and approached the surrender by asking Sakomizu what he thought when news of the Hiroshima bomb arrived:

A. When this news came on the morning of the 7th I called the Prime Minister on the phone and reported the announcement. Everyone in the government and even in the military knew that if the announcement were true, no country could carry on a war. Without the atomic bomb it would be impossible for any country to defend itself against a nation which had the weapon. The chance had come to end the war. It was not necessary to blame the military side, the manufacturing people, or anyone else—just the atomic bomb. It was a good excuse. Someone said that the atomic bomb was the kamikaze to save Japan.

Q. How long do you think the war would have continued if the atomic bomb had not been used?

A. We had already asked the Russians to intercede, and we could expect that they would eventually give us some answer. If it had been unfavorable there was just one way to bring peace and that was to broadcast directly to the United States. But it would have been difficult to find a good chance to do so. I think you can understand. Suzuki tried to find a chance to stop the war and the atom bomb gave him that chance.

Most of Truman's critics assert that the atom bombs "changed no minds" in Japan. The charge is false, and also irrelevant. The Bomb created a situation in which the peace party and Emperor could prevail.

Admiral Baron Kantaro Suzuki, Premier at the time of the surrender, was interrogated on December 26. Here, of all people, was the witness who might have been able to dislodge any lingering support for the early surrender hypothesis. Unfortunately, the civilian leadership of USSBS was back in Washington, D.C. Generals Anderson and Gardner, civilians Paul Baran and Burton Fisher asked the questions. Suzuki was responsive, even to questions about his instructions from the Emperor. About his plight when he became Premier (on April 7, 1945) Suzuki said:

It seemed to me unavoidable that in the long run Japan would be almost destroyed by air attack so that merely on the basis of the B-29s alone I was convinced that Japan should sue for peace. On top of the B-29 raids came the atomic bomb, immediately after the Potsdam Declaration, which was just one additional reason for giving in and was a very good one and gave us the opportune moment to make open negotiations for peace. I myself on the basis of the B-29 raids felt that the cause was hopeless. The Supreme War Council, up to the time the atomic bomb was dropped, did not believe that Japan could be beaten by air attack alone. They also believed that the United States would land and not attempt to

bomb Japan out of the war. On the other hand there were many prominent people who did believe that the United States could win the war by
just bombing alone. However the Supreme War Council, not believing
that, had proceeded with the one plan of fighting a decisive battle at
the landing point and was making every possible preparation to meet
such a landing. They proceeded with that plan until the atomic bomb was
dropped, after which they believed the United States would no longer
attempt to land when it had such a superior weapon-so at that point they
decided that it would be best to sue for peace.

NO CLEARER, NOR MORE PROBATIVE, STATEMENT EXISTS GIVING THE REASON WHY JAPAN SURRENDERED WHEN SHE DID.

Major General Tatsuhiko Takashima, Chief of Staff of the 12th Area
army defending the Kanto Plan was interrogated on November 24. This
interrogation is a forecast of Armageddon. Takashima knew every detail of the plan by which his army confidently expected to drive General
Douglas MacArthur out of Honshu with intolerable casualties. Here was
a leader full of bushido and self-confidence, who obviously believed he
had been sold out by cowardly civilians:

Q. How were these troops protected in their positions on the coast?
A. The majority of them were in caves. In a local area, they were of the
   fox-hole type. By August we had communications trenches between
   squads. We intended to have them between platoons by November.
   The best caves could withstand a hit by one- or two-ton bombs. By
   August the total length of under-cover emplacements equaled the
   length of the shore line in the area.
Q. What is your estimate of the success you would have had, if we had
   attacked as you estimated?
A. I think we would have been successful and won. We would have succeeded in driving you off the beaches.
Q. Did the dropping of the atomic bombs change your mind in any
   way?
A. No. There was no change in our plans. Its greatest effect was on

civilians. It did not affect the army. Our men were dug in deeply enough to protect themselves. There was only one area where we couldn't get under cement.

This startling interrogation was conducted by two American Colonels and a Captain. No high-ranking member of the Survey was present. Takashima belittled atomic bombs, but there can be no doubt that surrender was the last thing on his agenda.

Rear Admiral Toshitane Takata, Air Specialist on the Naval General Staff, was interrogated twice. Had Takata realized the war was lost when the Americans took Saipan and could then bomb Japan? Yes, he realized then that the bombers could destroy Japan's industrial capacity, "but our hope was that, if we could destroy the invasion fleet when it came to actually land in Japan—although Japan could not win the war—it could hold out indefinitely for any number of years...."

Rear Admiral Sadatoshi Tomioka, operations Officer of the Naval General Staff after November 1944. Tomioka was conversant with Japanese intelligence and planning, and heavily involved in the defenses of Iwo Jima, Okinawa, and Kyushu. After the fall of Saipan, he did not think that Japan would win the war: "Our only hope was that we could discourage you by inflicting great damage on your forces. We estimated that we would destroy 30-40% of the initial assaulting forces when you hit the homeland." He expected the invasion of Kyushu in July or early August 1945, since, "We felt that your home front pressure would require you to move fast and try to end the war as quickly as possible.... You couldn't bomb us into submission, I thought, and therefore you would have to land on the home island." No hint of early surrender here.

Lieutenant General Tadakazu Wakamatsu, Chief of Staff of the 2nd General Army (Hiroshima) until July 1945, then Vice-Minister of War, was interrogated on November 7. He was candid about Japan's liabilities in 1945: "Japan expected to repel only the first wave of the invasion. They had no hopes of repelling the second and third waves, but planned to retreat to the mountainous section."

Early surrender? With no atom bombs, no Russians, no invasion? Careful inspection of the "testimony of the surviving Japanese leaders involved"—even that incomplete sample available to USSBS during its two short months in 1945-shows only Kido supporting Nitze and everyone else stating that Japan would have fought on indefinitely. When would Japan have surrendered without the Bomb and the Russians? The *only* credible answer is that given by Robert Butow when Freeman Dyson asked him about it: "The Japanese leaders themselves do not know the answer to that question."

USSBS conclusions suffer not just from Nitze's preconceived opinions about early surrender, but from the worst features of instant history. There was no time for thoughtful investigators familiar with Japanese history to formulate really probing questions, nor to assimilate what was learned in early interviews and use it to sharpen later ones. It was precisely this opportunity that Robert Butow maximized in his 1954 study of Japan's surrender, still in 1995 the best source.

There is not room here for an extensive review of the data USSBS did *not* gather, but one example is suggestive. The Historical Division, Military Intelligence Section of the Far East Command, U.S. Army, on December 23, 1949, interrogated Lieutenant Colonel Masao Inaba, who was chief of the Budget Branch, Military Affairs Bureau, Japanese War Ministry, in 1945. Inaba was active in a group determined to "fight on with unshakable determination" even as the cabinet was wrestling with terms of surrender on August 11. This group usurped the authority of War Minister Anami and published a fire-breathing proclamation in the newspapers calling on all Japanese to "eat grass, swallow dirt, and lie in the fields" if necessary to destroy the arrogant enemy.

The most consequential of the Pacific Survey's publications, *Japan's Struggle to End the War*, says nothing of the attempted coup d'état by Inaba and five other junior military officers on the evening of August 14-15, the night before the Emperor's surrender rescript was broadcast. This is an amazing omission. Butow devotes a sixteen-page chapter to *Longest Day* (Tokyo and Palo Alto, 1968), which is primarily about that specific event. One can understand its omission from *Japan's Struggle* only by assuming that the attempted coup demonstrates such a fanatical resistance to surrender that Nitze's counter-factual becomes unbelievable.

Even as late as August 14, dissident forces seized the Imperial Compound, assassinated the commander of the Imperial Guards, Lieutenant General Takeshi Mori, attempted to block the Emperor's broadcast, attempted to assassinate Premier Suzuki, and burned Suzuki's residence when they could not find him. There were other rebellions even after the Emperor's broadcast. Surrender, in August 1945, barely came off. It was not just around the corner absent Hiroshima, Nagasaki, and a rumored third atomic bomb due on Tokyo.

In addition to ignoring the final convulsion, *Japan's Struggle* contains errors that more time, greater care, and less bias would have prevented. All the errors reinforce the early surrender hypothesis. *Japan's Struggle* says (page 3) that when Tojo fell and Koiso replaced him in July 1944, 'Koiso received an Imperial admonition to give Japan's situation a 'fundamental reconsideration' looking to the termination of the war." Butow refutes this. *Japan's Struggle* states on page 5 that "The Emperor on his own initiative in February 1945 had a series of interviews with the senior statesmen whose consensus was that Japan faced certain defeat and should seek peace at once." Grand Chamberlain Fujita's notes, taken at these interviews, show these claims to be false.

Japan's Struggle says that Prince Konoye told the Survey that he had secret instructions from the Emperor in July 1945 to negotiate through the Russians for "peace at any price" (pages 7, 13). No such statement appears in the transcripts of the Konoye interviews, and the testimony of Foreign Minister Togo contradicts it. *Japan's Struggle* (pages 12-13) states that in April 1945 when Suzuki was made Prime Minister, the Emperor told him to make peace at any price, and that this was known to all members of his cabinet. This is wholly false.

Japan's Struggle admits that the atomic bombs foreshortened the war and expedited the peace (page 12), but the basic thrust of the document faithfully reflects Nitze's pre-investigation opinion. Conventional bombing and naval blockade are alleged to have set in motion an irrevocable course toward surrender. Starvation was the issue; atomic spectacles were irrelevant.

Perhaps more debilitating than these biases and errors, however, was the failure of USSBS to obtain and use the massive *pre-surrender* intelligence gathered by MacArthur's ULTRA (see note below) code breakers. Whatever testimony USSBS took after the war, however desolate the bombed-out Japanese landscape, the probative value of these intercepted Japanese communications during the last months of the war as to Japanese willingness and ability to resist American invasion of Kyushu (operation OLYMPIC) overwhelms all other indices of Japanese intentions.

The feeble and vague attempts of the Japanese peace party to negotiate a favorable armistice through Moscow are well known. The belligerent and successful efforts of the Japanese military to prepare for the "decisive battle of the homeland" lay buried in the decrypted cable traffic.[4]

Professor Newman concludes his condemnation of Nitze, USSBS, *Japan's Struggle:* "USSBS concocted a scenario in which "Japan's Decision to Surrender" simply took a little time. The peace party had to beat down the militarists. It would have happened soon, atom or no.

There is no basis for this scenario in USSBS interrogations. No one can ever know how long the war would have gone on.

---

[4]Note: The only extensive study of this ULTRA traffic is Edward Drea's, *MacArthur's Ultra: Code-breaking and the War against Japan*, 1942-1945, Lawrence, Kansas, 1992.

Chapter 24
U.S. Lives Saved by the Atomic Bomb

would like to encapsulate what we now know about the number of casualties the United States would have incurred had President Truman not ordered the use of the atomic bomb, and we had to invade Japan.

Look at the maps and military involved. Review all of the books and data on casualty estimates from General Marshall, Admiral Leahy, Admiral Nimitz, The Joint Chiefs of Staff, Secretary of War Stimson, General MacArthur, President Truman's books and letters, and all others (post war) giving casualty estimates of 250,000 and more, with General Marshall, Stimson, Truman's papers and others going to 1,000,000. (*Signals Intelligence*—page 26.)

Remember the millions of Japanese men with military experience, men, women, boys and girls organized with a fight to the death suicide mentality; thousands of suicide kamikaze planes, suicide submarines, suicide manned torpedoes, civilians (women, boys and girls included) taught to kill with suicide bombs and hand grenades. Factor in the elaborate fortifications, bunkers, pillboxes with connecting tunnels.

Then you should accept the conclusion of a General more qualified than the Joint Chiefs of Staff, General MacArthur, General Marshall and all the leaders mentioned in this book, to give an estimate of casualties in the proposed invasion of Japan.

GENERAL Ray Davis fought with the First Marine Division on Guadalcanal, the first vicious land battle with the Japanese, then on Peleliu (earning Navy Cross, Purple Heart) another vicious bloody battle with the Japanese. He also fought with the Marine Corps at the Chosin Reservoir in the Korean War where he earned the Medal of Honor. He also served as Commanding General of the Third Marine Division in Vietnam, being considered one of the great field commanders of all time.

To complete his knowledge of the Japanese, he went to Japan after their surrender, representing the Marine Corps, to examine the defenses, fortifications, bunkers, pillboxes, land mines, suicide planes, and suicide submarines the Japanese had assembled.

According to General Davis and many others, when viewed after the Japanese surrender, the intricate death traps and defenses were even more deadly than they had imagined.

Listen:

> *"In predicting casualties for the invasion of Japan, my experience on Peleliu and my knowledge of the great number of divisions of U.S. military personnel, (including all six (6) divisions of the U.S. Marine Corps) together with my observation (post-war) of the awesome defenses on Kyushu and Honshu, which would be encountered in the invasion, leads me to believe that any casualty estimates would have to be in the 1 million to 2 million range."*

"Being in the initial 'Olympic Operations' assault force and in the initial 'Coronet Operation' assault force, it has been reasonably predicted (and I sadly agree) that the Marine Corps Force would have ceased to exist, after the invasion."

—*General Ray Davis*

Chapter 25
Bibliography – Valid or Counterfactual

Professor Robert P. Newman used the word, counterfactual, for the distortions used by Nitze and the other revisionists. Professor Newman is more diplomatic than I tend to be.

In the bibliography section I have listed those authors who I tell you are credible historians, and next listed are those I assure you have distorted history because of their agenda.

The revisionists all use specific and indefensible figures as the basis for their conclusion as to the number of U.S. casualties to be expected in the planned invasion of Japan, to begin November 1, 1945, viz: 20,000 to 46,000 (maximum). In the main text it will be shown that these figures, if ever having any valid basis, were for many months before the atomic bomb was used and did not, could not, take into account the rapid influx of Japanese divisions into Kyushu, escalating their troop strength from 100,000 in 1944 to about 228,000 on April 28, 1945; then to almost 600,000 (Central Intelligence Agency—*Signals of Intelligence*—see pages 23 and 46) by August 4, 1945

The revisionist blatant distortion of expected casualties will be readily apparent to any reader looking at the maps of Kyushu showing the number of U.S. troops invading and the increased Japanese troop strength there. Add to this the terrible invasion conditions of Kamikaze planes, suicide bombs by women and children, suicide submarines, suicide-manned torpedoes, and underground defenses, (explained in the main text) and the revisionist low casualty figures are even more absurd.

Specific intelligence figures for Japanese strength on Kyushu began with the April 28, 1945 figure of 228,000 because on April 3, 1945 the Joint Chiefs of Staff directed General Douglas MacArthur, Commander in Chief of US Army Forces in the Pacific (CINCPAC) and Admiral Chester Nimitz, Commander in Chief of the Pacific Fleet and the Pacific Ocean area (CINCPOA) to develop plans and begin preparations for an invasion of Kyushu.

The readers of this book need to read and digest one major flaw (among many) in the reasoning of Gar Alperovitz, probably the most vocal and most quoted of the atom bomb revisionists. On page eleven of the introduction in his book, *Atomic Diplomacy* (First Edition—1965, Second Edition—1985), he says: "Note carefully, first that the invasion of Japan, which was estimated to cost between 500,000 and 1,000,000 lives, was not scheduled until the Spring of 1946, roughly eight months after the Potsdam Conference and the bombing of Hiroshima on August 6th. As we shall see, there is little doubt that President Truman and his top advisors knew at the time the full invasion of Japan was extremely unlikely. The real issue was whether the war could be ended before November 1st, the date fixed for an INITIAL PRELIMINARY LANDING on the island of Kyushu. Again, note carefully, this was scheduled to occur three full months after the meeting at Potsdam, and one week shy of three months after Hiroshima was bombed...."

To call Hiroshima a "preliminary landing" shows he has absolutely no understanding of the Kyushu invasion plans or of World War II, or of war.

Kyushu WAS the invasion of Japan, nothing preliminary about it: 766,700 U.S. military. The Normandy landing in France, D-day in Europe was 150,000 troops.

After thirty years of research, Alperovitz persisted in this distortion of history in his later book, *Hiroshima, the Decision to use the Atomic Bomb*. On page 579, to criticize the Interim Committee for recommending the use of the atomic bomb, he immensely magnifies his misunderstanding of the war, and I quote: "few would likely have caught the fact that the invasion which might cause major casualties could not have taken place before the spring of 1946 and that when the interim committee met there was still five months left before even a November landing might possibly occur on Kyushu." Implying (actually saying) NO MAJOR CASUALTIES ON KYUSHU; with well over 600,000 Japanese (and still increasing) opposing 766,700 U.S. Military invaders.

Chapter 26
Revisionists

Revisionists led by Gar Alperovitz and Peter Kuznick base their argument that the Japanese were ready to surrender on the fact that the U.S. knew of the Emperor's Initiative—"U.S. officials knew first hand of the Emperor's initiative (to end the war)," page 237—Gar Alperovitz' book, *Hiroshima, the Decision to use the Atomic Bomb.*

There is nothing new, startling or earth shattering about this being known to the U.S. thru Ultra (magic) intercepts. Foreign Minister Shigenori Togo, on behalf of the Emperor, was urging Ambassador Sato, Japan's Ambassador to the Soviet Union, to prevail on the Russian Government to receive Prince Konoye to discuss ending the war. –Bruce Lee (Sato, page 533, 534)

Revisionists equate wanting to—"discuss ending the war" with "surrender." Nothing could be further from the truth.

Revisionists should acknowledge Ambassador Sato, his attempts to talk to Foreign Minister Molotov to persuade him to have the Russian government (Stalin) receive Prince Konoye "to discuss peace" and Sato's feeling that Japan should go to the United Nations to seek peace. (See *Marching Orders*, Bruce Lee, page 540.)

Far from telling Washington that the Emperor is ready to surrender, the Magic (Ultra) intercepts show that Japan's leaders refuse Sato's advice and want to pursue talks through Russia. This proves conclusively that Japan wanted to discuss "terms for peace" as opposed to surrender.

Very important also had been an Ultra intercept from Sato: "as for seeing Molotov, I would particularly like to be informed whether our Imperial Government has a concrete and definite plan for terminating the war; otherwise, I will make no immediate request for an interview." (*Marching Orders*, Bruce Lee, page 533.) As of July 30, 1945 the Japanese government has no plan for ending the war.

To confirm that at this point Japan had no plan to give up the war. Stanley Weintraub in his book, *The Last Great Victory*, page 289 quotes Togo to Sato "no matter how hard I may try to persuade the military to hold direct negotiations with the Americans or British, I have no doubt whatsoever that they will refuse to listen. Therefore, we must attempt to negotiate through the Soviet Union, because there seems no other way to terminate the war."

All Revisionist writers cited in this book, — Alperovitz, Kuznick, Lifton, Kai Bird, Bernstein, et al, rely mainly on one writer, one source (U.S.S.B.S. Paul Nitze).

They all parrot and rely on Nitze for their "ready to surrender" "Japanese were beaten and knew it" "Japanese were in the MOOD to surrender" (See Alperovitz—*Hiroshima: the Decision to use the Atomic Bomb*, page 477) (Nitze's writing in U.S.S.B.S. reports, particularly "Japan's struggle")

In addition to Professor Robert Newman's manuscript, completely refuting Paul Nitze's "Early Surrender" claim (detailed in this book), we know that Nitze, Alperovitz, Kuznick, et al. completely ignore the fact that at the time the atomic bomb was dropped (though the Emperor could, in theory, determine the end of the war) the Supreme War Council (Big Six) and from August, 1944 until the end of the war, did, in fact control the course of the war, and specifically, whether and when to end it. The Supreme War Council:

(1) Premier: Admiral Baron Kantaro Suzuki, Imperial Japanese Navy
(2) Foreign Minister Shigenori Togo
(3) War Minister: Army General Korechika Anami
(4) Navy Minister: Admiral Mitsumasa Yonai
(5) Chief of Army General Staff: General Yoshijiro Umezu
(6) Chief of Navy General Staff: Admiral Teijoro Toyoda

Whatever Nitze, Alperovitz, Kuznick, et al. say about Japanese "willingness to surrender," "Emperor ready to surrender," "mood of the Japanese was to surrender," these arguments are trumped and obliterated by what we know of the operation of this Supreme War Council.

The Japanese had received the Potsdam Proclamation on July 27, 1945, and the Supreme War Council had, through Premier Suzuki, announced that Japan would "mokusatsu" the Proclamation, literally "kill it with silence" "treat it with silent contempt" "ignore it" as a "thing of no great value." (See *Japan's Decision to Surrender*—Robert Butow, page 145, 146—also *The Last Great Victory*, page 289). Mokusatsu is discussed at length elsewhere in this book. From that day until August 14, 1945, this War Council was divided 3 to 3 as to whether to surrender under the Potsdam Proclamation. (Butow—page 201 and *The Last Great Victory*, page 289).

On August 14, 1945 the council had asked the Emperor to convene an Imperial Conference to resolve the difference between the Council members: with Suzuki, Togo, Yonai for accepting the Potsdam Declaration, and Umezu, Anami, Toyoda against.

The Emperor in a lengthy statement announced his agreement with Premier Suzuki, Togo and Yonai and that they should proceed to end the war. Without any further discussion by the Big Six it was understood they would proceed to implement the peace process (*Japan's Decision to Surrender*, page 206, 207 and 208).

The Council then prepared the Imperial Rescript announcing Japan's capitulating; Japan's ministers in Switzerland and Sweden were to transmit the decision to the Allied Powers. The next day August 15, 1945 the Emperor broadcast his rescript to the Japanese people (Butow- P. 208, 209).

What Alperovitz, Kuznick and all the Revisionists do not discuss is the fact that General Anami, General Umezu, Admiral Toyoda, the die-hard "fight-to-the-finish" one-half of the War Council, insisted on four conditions of surrender, as opposed to Suzuki, Admiral Yonai, Foreign Minister Togo only insisting on preservation of the Imperial House. Until the Imperial Conference August 14, 1945 when the Emperor finalized his direction to the War Council to end the war, Umezu, Anami, Toyoda insisted on three more conditions: viz, (1) that there be no security occupation of Japan (2) that disarmament and demobilization be left in Japanese hands, (3) War criminals be tried by Japanese Tribunals. (See *Signals Intelligence*, Central Intelligence Agency Monograph by MacEachin, page 36—*Codename Downfall*, page 331—*The Last Great Victory*, by Weintraub, page 505—*Japan's Decision to Surrender*, by Professor Butow, page 207).

{These three conditions would *never* be granted by the Allies.}

Chapter 27

Revisionsts: Books and Articles

These are listed separately, because I want readers to realize that their criticisms of the use of the atom bomb (to end World War II against Japan) are all totally without credibility.

WHY THEY HAVE NO CREDIBILITY:

(1) Their false deceptive (maybe dishonest) casualty estimates for U.S. forces in the planned invasion of Japan.

They all insist, and repeat over and over in their writings, that the casualties in the proposed invasion of Japan, would have been 20,000 to 63,000 (maximum).

Sad for a writer who claims to be a historian to repeatedly use these figures, blatantly disregarding the unquestioned numbers of U.S. military troops scheduled to assault Kyushu in Operation Olympic. November 1, 1945 (i.e. 766,700 Marines and Army units) with Kyushu being defended by approximately 600,000 Japanese. This number was increasing every day with every indication it could reach 900,000 by November 1, 1945. (Charles Willoughby, General McArthur's Intelligence Chief predicts this number in a July 28, 1945 memo: page 194 of Professor Newman's Pacific Historical Review Article; also cited in Douglas MacEachin's *Signals Intelligence* Manuscripts. This 600,000 estimate was at the end of July 1, 1945.)

Look at these figures: 30,000 Japanese defenders on Saipan (almost all killed) and 17,000 U.S. casualties. Then Okinawa with almost all of the 107,000 Japanese defenders killed, with 68,000 U.S. casualties. Add the 100,000 Okinawans killed and simple arithmetic will tell you 600,000 Japanese troops defending Kyushu, facing 766,700 invading U.S. troops would inflict huge casualties many times above the 63,000 these revisionists grudgingly fix as the maximum to be envisioned in the invasion of Japan.

You must note that, shockingly, the 63,000 casualty estimate is for the entire Japanese home island invasion. This would include Operation Coronet (March 1, 1946) on the island of Honshu.

With some 2,000,000 Japanese troops defending Honshu (to quote Dr. Thomas Sowell, Stanford University Emeritus Profession, commenting on these low revisionists estimates) "it would be funny if it were not so sick."

I have tried to cover these casualty estimates in credible detail elsewhere.

(2) The Revisionists can have no credibility as they, without any factual basis, assert that the Japanese would probably surrender by November 1, 1945 and assuredly by December 31, 1945.

This assertion was made by one man, Paul Nitze, based on one reluctant statement by one Japanese, Marquis Koichi Kido, Lord of the Privy Seal and confidant of the Emperor (See main text).

Nitze was speaking for the United States Strategic Bombing Survey in their report of the effect on bombing against the Japanese. The report was written and controlled by Nitze and was in fact the unswerving opinion he formed immediately after arriving in the Pacific Theatre from the European Theatre. Nitze was the principal author of the survey's final report. (See his book, *From Hiroshima to Glasnot* , also USSBS report).

This faulty conclusion is discussed in the main text and Robert P. Newman's manuscript shows that these conclusions were without any basis in fact.

Gar Alperovitz, Atomic Diplomacy-1965 (second edition-1985)
Author: *The Decision to Use the Atomic Bomb*

Dr. Alperovitz is a historian and political economist and has been a guest scholar at Brookings Institute and has been a guest professor at Notre Dame University and has written other books and many articles on the atomic bomb.

Alperovitz makes extremely false assertions concerning the number of casualties predicted in the event of an invasion of Japan. He asserts as fact on page 515 of his book, *The Decision to Use the Atomic Bomb* that, "—avoiding a FULL 1946 INVASION might save in the range of 46,000." You will note that I have highlighted 'full 1946 invasion' as it demonstrates Alperovitz' lack of real knowledge of the invasion plans or an invasion landing that would be far larger than the Normandy landing in Europe (when the Allies invaded France to begin to defeat Hitler's Nazi armies). Alperovitz refers to it as 'preliminary'. What a Historian?

He quotes General Marshall as estimating 31,000 casualties in the first thirty days of the Kyushu landing (an early prediction). These figures are completely out of date considering the number of Japanese on Kyushu on August 6, 1945 and predicted for November 1, 1945.

Barton Bernstein, Professor of History, Stanford University

Professor Bernstein, based on a faulty interpretation of a June 18, 1945 entry in the diary of Admiral William D. Leahy, the President's Chief of Staff, determined that the U.S. casualties would be a maximum of 63,000. This is a figure that all of these revisionist professors adhered to and repeated over and over.

Professor Bernstein was responsible for the Air and Space Museum Director, Martin Harwit placing these figures in the failed *Enola Gay* exhibit in 1995. Professor Bernstein was one of the activists concerning the flawed *Enola Gay* exhibit of 1995.

Robert J. Lifton and Greg Mitchell
Authors of: *Hiroshima in America: 50 Years of Denial*

This book is one of the more elaborate and caustic critics of the atomic bomb and personally of President Harry Truman. Lifton also wrote, *Death in Life: Survivors of Hiroshima* and other books. Lifton is a distinguished professor of psychiatry and psychology and John Jay College and Graduate School of the City University of New York, and Director of the Center on Violence and Human Survival. Greg Mitchell is a renowned author, winner of the 1993 Goldsmith Book Prize from Harvard University, and editor of the *New York Times* magazine. He wrote many articles on the atomic bomb.

Hiroshima in America claims to be "a landmark psychological study," pronouncing that after the atomic bombs, "President Truman spent the rest of his life in the throws of unrealized guilt" (a diagnosis quite remarkable since neither author ever met Truman). These authors also declared that for fifty years all Americans have had a guilt complex about Hiroshima and the atomic bomb.

On page 34 of that book they scoff at a "belief in American virtue" in the war, that this meant, "we could occasionally use inhuman instruments—such as flame throwers". In this same paragraph they say our bombings in Europe and Japan should have been condemned.

Professor Lifton and Mr. Mitchell would not want to hear what Marines in all six Divisions of the Corps, and the infantry Army soldiers fighting in the Pacific, would say to an American critical of their use of flame throwers.

I have said in the past that, "this type thinking would have required us to use sterilized bullets."

The bias of these authors is also shown on page 119 of *Hiroshima in America*. Truman "decided to use atomic weapons on undefended cities because he was drawn to the power." (Note: as we had air superiority over the Japanese, we shouldn't attack any Japanese city??)

Peter Jennings, Author

Peter Jennings and Todd Brewster wrote, *The Century*, which is a running account of the history of the twentieth century and of course includes the period of time around World War II and the dropping of the atomic bomb.

In the main text we have discussed this book's distortion of the World War II account concerning the Japanese, the atrocities of the war, and how they were incorrect, particularly page 252.

Peter Jennings was also a national commentator for ABC television. He orchestrated a primetime program, "Hiroshima: Why the Bomb was Dropped" on July 27, 1995.

According to Gar Alperovitz's publisher, Knopf, his book, *The Decision to use the Atomic Bomb*, was the basis for the Jennings' special. Undoubtedly it was.

This television special was exactly according to the revisionists' opinion against the use of the Bomb and to show its bias; Jennings declined to use any material furnished to him and his producers by the Air Force

Association (this according to John T. Correll, editor in chief at *Air Force Magazine.*)

Peter Kuznick

Distinguished Professor and Historian at American University, Washington, D.C.; Director of Nuclear Studies Institute; Author and Lecturer on the atomic bomb and nuclear issues; Co-founder of the Nuclear Education Project at American University, Washington, D.C. and he organized the "Committee for National Discussion of Nuclear History and Current Policy"

Peter Kuznick and Mark Selden were in the middle of the battle concerning the *Enola Gay* Exhibit and protested vigorously any change in the exhibit.

Professor Kuznick conducts a seminar in Hiroshima, Japan every summer, concerning the fact that the atomic bomb was not needed.

Peter Kuznick is the author of several books and articles opposing the use of the atomic bomb.

Paul H. Nitze

Paul H. Nitze headed the United States Strategic Bombing Survey (USSBS) in Japan and its official reports were edited and controlled by him.

All of the "Early Surrender" authors derived their information and opinion from Paul H. Nitze and his USSBS final reports. The conclusions of those final reports were actually exploded by a manuscript of Professor Robert P. Newman, which is listed under his bibliography.

Paul Nitze wrote, *From Hiroshima to Glasnost: at the Center of Decision*, 1989.

He had a distinguished government career, Secretary of the Navy, 1963-1967. Later Deputy Secretary of Defense, member of the U.S. Delegation to the Strategic Arms Limitation Talks, and later Assistant Secretary of Defense for International Affairs.

He was (in this author's opinion, and that of Professor Newman and other historians) completely biased and incorrect in his statements concerning the atomic bomb.

Mark Selden

Mark Selden is a professor at Cornell University and coordinator of Japanese Focus concerning Japan and the Asia Pacific Theater. He, along with Peter Kuznick, has been extremely active in atom bomb demonstrations at the *Enola Gay* Exhibit and teaching and writing against the use of the atomic bomb. He is the author of several books on this subject.

Martin J. Sherwin

He is a professor of history at Dartmouth and Tuffs and along with Kai Bird Co-Chairman of "Historian's Committee for Open Debate on Hiroshima." Sherwin was an advisor to the Air and Space Museum on the *Enola Gay* Exhibit in 1994 and, to show his bias, he complained that the *Enola Gay* crew had shown "no remorse" for the atomic bomb mission.

Hiroshima Mayor Tadatoshi Akiba

Mayor Akiba was enlisted by Peter Kuznick as a coordinator of the Education Project of the Nuclear Studies Institute.

The Mayor came to participate with Peter Kuznick and his Committee in protesting the *Enola Gay* Exhibit, which was finally completed at the Dulles Airport.

John H. Coatsworthy, Professor at Harvard University; President of the American Historical Association

Coatsworthy criticized the changing of the flawed *Enola Gay* Exhibit and disparaged the "politicians, lobbying groups, editorial writers" and stated "why hire professional historians and curators to do an honest, thoughtful job when you really want propaganda?"

Coatsworthy, without examining the issues involved in the exhibit, was stating that these people proclaiming to be historians should be allowed to exhibit the *Enola Gay* as they saw fit.

AUTHOR'S NOTE:

These historically correct professors such as Alperovitz, Harwit, Crouch, Lifton, Kuznick, Kai Bird, Bernstein, Mitchell, Selden, Sherwin and others following Paul Nitze's flawed reasoning, in their 'early surrender' theory (and their low casualty estimate), obviously do not understand circumstantial evidence (or real evidence either).

The Mike Tyson-Evander Holyfield ear-biting incident reminded me of an illustration that we had in court some years ago, concerning circumstantial evidence. The case was a prosecution for "maiming another" and the principal witness had stated that the defendant 'bit off the ear of the other man'.

He had repeated this, but it seemed that he was not in position to actually see the ear being bitten. Seizing upon this, in an aggressive way, the defense counsel asked, "SO: you did not see him bite the ear off, did you? "No" said the witness.

"Oh, and yet you tell us that you know positively that the defendant bit off the man's ear?" asked the lawyer.

"Yes" said the witness.

Then the lawyer asked, "How can you say so positively that he bit the man's ear off if you did not see him bite it off?"

The witness: "I saw him spit it out."

CASE CLOSED.

The Japanese did not surrender until August 15, 1945, nine days after the first atom bomb was dropped on Hiroshima (August 6, 1945), and six days after the second atomic bomb was dropped on Nagasaki (August 9,1945). No other evidence needs to supplement the rest of the evidence that they were not 'ready to surrender'.

THEY WERE NOT READY TO SURRENDER.

Chapter 28
Credible Authors

These authors have demonstrated true factual research, as opposed to the obvious bias of the Revisionists listed previously.

Iris Chang

Rape of Nanking—"A *New York Times* Best Seller"

She had a journalism degree from the University of Illinois at Urbana, a graduate fellowship to the writing seminar program at Johns Hopkins University.

The foreword of Iris Chang's book, *Rape of Nanking* was by William C. Kirby, Professor of Modern Chinese History and Chairman of the Department of History at Harvard University. He acclaims it as the first comprehensive exam of the Rape of Nanking. Iris Chang did the most comprehensive research concerning the Rape of Nanking and also the atrocities in China. Iris Chang's speech for the R.N.R.C. mock tribunal at San Francisco City College on October 24, 2003 is placed in a chapter of this book as it is a comprehensive analysis of her findings and of the research she performed.

(This author attended that conference and spoke on the atomic bomb issue.)

Her work, research and the great discovery of the diary of John Rabe, a German business man who kept a detailed account of his observations while in Nanking at the time of the Rape of Nanking. The Yale Divinity School report precedes and verifies all of Iris Chang's research and findings.

American Missionary Eyewitnesses to the Nanking Massacre, 1937-1938 by the Yale Divinity School Library Occasional Publication No. 9.

This was issued in 1997 and edited by Martha Lund Smalley.

This publication by the Yale Divinity School Library describes the Nanking massacre as one of the greatest horrors in the annals of mankind and notes that despite the volume of evidence confirming the massacre the Japanese government still denies the undeniable and have even accused the United States of conspiring with China to fabricate the story in order to prove that the Japanese, being a cruel people, deserved the atomic bombing.

Comfort Women

A Pictorial Sketch edited by Poland Hung, Ed. D, published by: The Chinese Holocaust Museum of the United States, September, 2000.

This book pictures and describes the comfort women (more accurately described as sex slaves), which have been described in a number of books concerning the Japanese practice of capturing and sending women of all ages to be 'sex slaves' of the Japanese Imperial Army.

Ms. Gay MacDougal is notable on the women sex slave issue:

Ms. MacDougal was appointed by the United Nations sub-commission on human rights to complete a study on systematic rapes/slavery and slavery-like humanitarian and international criminal law frameworks.

Ms. MacDougal presented an analysis to the Japan Federation of Bar Associations Forum on June 2, 1999 in Tokyo: "The Analysis of Legal Responsibility of the Government of Japan on Comfort Women Issues and Recommendations to Solve it."

Ms. MacDougal's findings were detailed and summarized Japan's Military Sexual Slavery Practices During World War II.

Central Intelligence Agency-Signals Intelligence

The Final Months of the War with Japan: Signals Intelligence, U.S. Planning and the A. Bomb Decision by Douglas J. MacEachin (December, 1998)

This monograph produced under the auspices of CIA's "Center for Study of Intelligence" and the Harvard University "Program for Studies of Intelligence and Policy." The idea was to examine the role of signals intelligence in U.S. Military planning during the final stages of the war with Japan in 1945—particularly its contribution to planning for an allied invasion of the Japanese homeland. It expressed appreciation to Edward Drea "author of MacArthur's Ultra: (Code Breaking and the War against Japan)" a recognized military historian.

It covers and details all the issues facing President Truman and the United States in deciding to use the atomic bomb.

It particularly explodes the Revisionists (Alperovitz, Bernstein, Lifton, Kuznick, Harwit, Kai Bird) small casualty estimates (20,000 to 63,000 maximum) to U.S. Military in the planned invasion of Japan (*Operation Downfall*). It documents the huge increase of Japanese troop strength on Kyushu. It shows clearly that Japanese troop strength on Kyushu was 'three times' the original planning estimates. This is elaborated upon in the main text.

Dr. James Bryant Conant, President, Harvard University

Dr. Conant served on the Interim Committee appointed by the President to study the use of the atomic bomb and make recommendations. Dr. Conant recommended very positively the use of the Bomb by President Truman, along with the rest of the Interim Committee. Dr. Conant was instrumental in the writing of the account of the atomic bomb after the war by Secretary of State Stimson.

This is described in the main text, verifying the fact that the Bomb was proper and its use was positive.

John T. Correll

John T. Correll, at the time of the *Enola Gay* controversy at the National Air and Space Museum, 1995 was the Editor in Chief of the *Air Force Magazine*.

After the *Enola Gay* exhibit was modified to make it more reasonable at the National Air and Space Museum, the activists, (described in the text of this book) continued to criticize the display and criticize all those organizations which were responsible for changing the unpalatable exhibit originally designed for the *Enola Gay*. John Correll wrote a number of articles on the controversy, and in one of these, "The Activist and the *Enola Gay*" he showed clearly the untenable stance of the revisionists.

This was a well documented analysis of the *Enola Gay* controversy and demonstrated exactly how bizarre the conduct and the position of the revisionists, viz: Alperovitz, Kai Bird, Robert J. Lifton, Barton Bernstein, Peter Kuznick and others had been.

Gavan Daws

Author of, *Prisoners of the Japanese: POW's of World War II in the Pacific*, William Morrow and Company, Inc., New York.

Gavan Daws headed the historical research on the Pacific region at the Institute for Advanced Studies at the Australian National University and was elected to the Academy of Humanities in Australia. This book vividly describes the atrocities in starving, beating and killing prisoners of war by the Japanese.

Edward J. Drea

Author, *MacArthur's Ultra, Code Breaking and the War against Japan, 1942-1945.*

Edward Drea is Chief of the Research and Analysis Division at the U.S. Army Center of Military History in Washington, D.C. and author of the "1942 Japanese General Election." He is fluent in Japanese.

This book is a comprehensive examination of the use of Ultra, the material gathered from the Japanese code having been broken during World War II, and is a comprehensive study of how this information was used in fighting the war in the Pacific and the determination that the use of the atomic bomb to end the war correct.

Another book on THE RAPE OF NANKING
An Undeniable History in Pictures
Authors: James Yin and Shi Young

Foreword: By the Most Reverend Desmond M. Tutu
Anglican Archbishop of Capetown, South Africa
1984 Nobel Peace Prize Laureate

Contains more than 400 historical photographs of the massacre, many taken by the Japanese.
(We have used a number of these in this book.)

Herbert P. Bix

Japan's Delayed Surrender, (Hirohito and the Making of Modern Japan)

New York (Harper Collins—2000) Excellent book!

A Japan-based historian reveals Hirohito as a militarist involved with all the war activities of Japan, and verifies that Hirohito was shielded from his involvement by MacArthur and Japanese court officials fixing War Crimes Trials testimony.

Arnold Brackman

United Press Correspondent covered Class A War Crimes in Tokyo (War Minister Hideki Tojo being one of them).

Brackman reported testimony of many POW survivors: Camp Commandants had told them that they would be killed if Japan was invaded.

Book: *The Other Nuremberg*, New York: William, 1987

From the trials Brackman determined that the Nanking massacre and all Japanese atrocities were not the kind of isolated incidents common to wars, "It was deliberate. It was policy. It was known in Tokyo."

Professor Robert J. C. Butow

Japan's Decision to Surrender

Dr. Butow spent a year of research in Japan (1951-52).

Pacific Historical Review says, "His study will stand for many years as the definitive account of the men, the events, the policies, the politics, and pressures that contributed to the Japanese decision to surrender." Dr. Butow's book shows positively that the military leaders of Japan (the 'Big Six', with Prime Minister Shigemitsu, and a few others who controlled, along with the Emperor, the decision to surrender) did not agree to surrender until four days after the second atomic bomb August 9, 1945 (elaborated upon in the text).

James Bradley

Flags of our Fathers, a best seller about the battle of Iwo Jima where his father was one of the flag raisers on Mount Suribachi.

Flyboys, a later book on air power over Japan. It documents atrocities of the Japanese toward the end of the war on Chichi Jima, an island near

Iwo Jima, occupied by the Japanese Army and holding some captured American aviators. It specifically details the cannibalism of the Japanese on Chichi Jima and records the horrible details surrounding the Japanese Commander's order to execute Prisoner of War Lieutenant (j.g.) Floyd Hall for the purpose of cannibalism.

Linda Goetz Holmes

Unjust Enrichment, Stackpole Books, 2001 (How Japan's companies built postwar fortunes using American prisoners of war)' Excellent book on wartime conduct of the Japanese.

Dr. Edward Teller, one of the renowned scientists who created the atomic bomb, was quoted after the war as saying that the atomic bomb was unnecessary. Later, Dr. Teller was present at a gathering of survivors of Bataan, Corregidor and other prisoner of war camps in Japan, at the Admiral Nimitz Museum, Fredericksburg, Texas, in March 1995. There Dr. Teller changed his mind after listening to POW after POW tearfully thank him for saving their lives by use of the Bomb and showing Dr. Teller copies of the "Kill All Prisoners" order (shown in this book). Dr. Teller was so moved by the POWs thanking him for saving their lives that he expressed "an unshakeable fact—we had to aid the prisoners of war. We had to make peace."

Linda Goetz Holmes was present and reporting on this conference for The Australian, and furnished her account for this book.

Professor Sheldon Harris

Factories of Death; Japanese Biological Warfare, 1937-1945, and the American Cover-up, published—Routledge—London 1994—Later in the U.S. and Canada. Prof. Harris was Emeritus Professor, California State University, Northridge, California.

This book details the horrible activities of Unit 731, Unit 100, Unit Ei1644. These units produced cholera, anthrax, bubonic plague, glanders, typhoid, and other pathogens. These units were provided prisoners of war (Chinese, American, Australian and British) by the Japanese Imperial Army; as guinea pigs for the most diabolical inhuman experiments ever imagined. Also, Chinese men, women and children were randomly seized for these unthinkable experiments. The largest complex was Unit

731 near Harbin, China. Professor Harris spent a decade researching this horrible project. He describes the infecting of these humans, as guinea pigs, and then the routine vivisection of the victims while alive, practicing surgery to determine how the infected victim had been affected by the disease. The diabolical tests on live victims was, according to Professor Harris, "beyond science fiction." The Japanese infected thousands of wells of the Chinese to experiment with an epidemic scenario.

Professor Harris discloses the fact that Col. Ishii, the Commander of this project, and the thousands of his Army units who participated in the inhuman experiments from 1937 through 1945 were (in a Faustian bargain) given immunity from their war crimes by the U.S. through General Douglas MacArthur's headquarters. Not one of this group, who participated in some of the most hideous war crimes in all history, was tried as a war criminal.

Dr. Lester Tenney
My Hitch in Hell
Professor of Finance-Arizona State University (Retired)

Lester Tenney wrote about surviving the Bataan Death March, being beaten and almost dying on the march, while witnessing the torture and killing of many of his fellow soldiers, as well as Filipino soldiers, on the inhuman Death March.

He pointed out the Japanese military command order issued in Manila, April, 1942 after the surrender of about 12,000 American and 70,000 Filipino soldiers. Quote: "Every troop which fought against our army on Bataan should be wiped out thoroughly whether he surrendered or not, and any American captive who is unable to continue marching all the way to the concentration camp should be put to death in the area 200 meters off the highway."

Tenney gives a vivid mind-searing account of the unbridled, brutal "recreational" killing by the Japanese troops along the 65-mile Death March of 12 deadly inhuman days.

This 12-day march of torture was followed by his being sent to Japan as a slave-laborer for Mitsui Corporation. This excruciating, painful slave-labor existed in the Mitsui coal mine for 3 ½ years until his liberation in September, 1945.

Lester Tenney weighed 185 pounds before the war and weighed 101 pounds when he was liberated. This was the exact experience of every POW, as only a "lucky" few survived. Speaking with Lester Tenney, Mel Rosen, Frank Bigelow, Edward Jackfert and several other POW's, I realized not only how lucky they were but it seemed an old phrase I've heard applied to all of them. "They were as tough as a one-eyed alley cat."

Kinue Tokudome
Japan Policy Research Institute (Working Paper No. 82)
Title: *POW Forced Labor Lawsuits against Japanese Companies*

Japanese author Kinue Tokudome has written extensively on the subject of justice for victims of Japanese war crimes in journals such as *Ushio*, *Ronza*, *Gaiko Forum*, and the *Asahi Shimbun* (Japanese Publishers). During the year 2000 she held an Abe Fellowship for research on reparations for war crimes at the Institute of Social Science, University of Tokyo.

This remarkable young Japanese lady is one of the more outstanding people who are contributing to a true history of the Japanese and their history before and during World War II.

Karen Parker, Lawyer (Juris Doctor)

Karen Parker lives in San Francisco, California and practices in International, Human Rights and Humanitarian (armed conflict) Law.

International Law of Human Rights Association, Strasburg, France.

She is an expert in Human Rights Law and particularly as it applies to the "sex slaves" (comfort women) enslaved by the Japanese Imperial Army prior to and during World War II. She, most properly, designated them as war-rape victims, they being women of all ages, and girls as young as 12 years of age taken from their homes in Korea, China, Dutch East Indies, Taiwan, Malaysia, Burma and the Philippines. Then distributed like animals to service the Japanese Imperial Army. Karen Parker has tirelessly represented many of these war-rape victims in lawsuits against Japan, seeking compensation and acknowledgment for the atrocities by the Japanese Government. Small compensation has been obtained along with some significant rulings (Japanese courts) that declare the "sex-slave traffic" by the Japanese Imperial Army actually occurred. It is impossible to get adequate compensation or a complete acknowledgement by the Japanese government. This great lawyer's work validates the claims of the war-rape victims with only a few still alive to testify.

Peter Li
Japanese War Crimes (The Search for Justice)

Peter Li has been editor-in-chief of *East Asia: An International Quarterly* and Associate Professor of Asian Studies and Comparative Literature at Rutgers University, New Brunswick, New Jersey.

Professor Li has assembled a compendium of many of the factual accounts of the atrocities of the Japanese Imperial Army, and further proves the validity of the atrocity claims. His book is a strong argument for the Japanese to acknowledge for history their World War II war crimes and atrocities dating from before 1931.

Mike Honda, U.S. Congressman, San Jose, California

Mike Honda (whom I met, listened to, and admire) is an American of Japanese descent, whose parents and relatives suffered in the World War II internment of Japanese-Americans. He has introduced resolutions in Congress to call on the Japanese to stop denying the atrocities in China, Southeast Asia, Korea and all of World War II. He has campaigned for Japan to admit the sex-slave issue, compensate the victims, and correct their history books. He was active in the Redress movement that persuaded the U.S. Government to acknowledge the internments of Japanese-Americans in World War II as being wrong and providing some compensation for the wrongs.

He has been just as active in the campaign to have Japan acknowledge its atrocities from prior to 1931 through the end of World War II in September, 1945. He deserves a special place of honor among those who seek justice concerning Japanese World War II atrocities.

James Mackay
Betrayal in High Places
Published by Tasman Books, Auckland, New Zealand, 1996

This is an account of a World War II -Fleet Air Arm Lieutenant of New Zealand, named James Gowing Godwin. Godwin was aboard a ship sunk by the Japanese, March 9, 1944 and was a POW for the remainder of the war, until September, 1945. Godwin kept a diary of the cruelty of the Japanese to him and the cruelty, starvation and murder of POWs by the Japanese. Godwin learned the Japanese language while a POW.

When the war ended he was assigned to the Second Australian War Crimes Section in Tokyo, under the jurisdiction of General Douglas MacArthur. Godwin was commissioned as an Army Captain, Australian Intelligence.

Godwin participated in investigating and examining some of the most heinous war criminals of the Japanese Imperial Army including a number who had participated in the cannibalism of New Zealand and Allied military captives.

This book is a valuable source for showing the orders from MacArthur's headquarters in granting immunity to Col. Ishii and his diabolical warfare army units. Then in the final and critical stages of investigation of some of the worst War Criminals ever (admitted cannibals, those who sadistically beheaded New Zealand, Australian and Allied military captives, those who tortured and killed civilian and military captives) an order came to terminate the investigations and release the depraved Japanese War criminals. Even more inexplicable was the order from MacArthur's headquarters to destroy all the documents concerning these most inhuman war crimes ever.

This book is a most valuable source for acts of some of these major war criminals, because Captain Godwin kept a number of the records of the war criminals he had interrogated and investigated.

In a small way this will help to preserve some of history, so blatantly destroyed and overlooked, involving the war crimes of the Japanese Imperial Army; some of the most abominable in the history of the world.

Examples are used in the main text

Bruce Lee

Marching Orders—The Untold Story of World War II, (Crown, 1995).

Bruce Lee was the First Editor in Chief of *Reader's Digest Press* and a White House Correspondent for *Reader's Digest*. As a well-trained *Newsweek* researcher, he spent 13 months (1962-1963) in U.S. Army archives in Alexandria, Virginia researching World War II in the Pacific.

This is an excellent book on the last days of WWII and a well detailed account of the huge casualty estimates expected in the planned invasion of Japan. Among other facts, he quotes Samuel Halpern, one of the OSS planners in Washington helping with the top secret planning for the invasion of Japan. Halpern was repeatedly told that 500,000 casualties were expected in the first thirty days and that for a ninety-day campaign 1.5 million casualties could be easily envisaged for the invasion and occupation of Japan (*Marching Orders*, page 489).

GLOBAL ALLIANCE TO PRESERVE THE HISTORY OF WORLD WAR II IN ASIA

Global Alliance is a large group of organizations devoted to correcting the poor historical accounts of the Sino-Japanese War which began before 1931, the Japanese occupation of Korea (1910), the Japanese conduct during those wars and World War II in the Pacific against the United States of America.

The Alliance was formed in 1995 around the time of the *Enola Gay* controversy at the National Air and Space Museum, and the many distortions of World War II history occurring about that year, which was the fifty-year celebration of the end of World War II. (The celebration was dampened by the ultra-revisionists who used that time to blame the U.S. for being heartless in using the atomic bomb).

The largest of the chapters of the Alliance was the Center For Internee Rights, composed of civilian internees and prisoners of war of the Japanese (and sympathizers, one being this author). The next largest group was "Alliance to Preserve the Truth of the Sino-Japanese War" headquartered in San Jose, California.

Bataan Death March survivors, Hell Ships survivors, Corregidor survivors, Comfort Women (sex slaves) survivors, Wake and Guam survivors, and many others belong to the Alliance, which has large chapters in Toronto, and Vancouver, Canada; Los Angeles, San Francisco, Washington, D.C., Beijing and Shanghai-Peoples Republic of China; Taipei, Taiwan; and many other cities.

The Alliance has a major conference twice a year at Beijing, Toronto,

San Francisco, Shanghai and numerous special meetings at all of these places at intervals.

Most of the credible authors named in the bibliography section have been members of the Alliance and have worked on its projects.

Ignatius Ding, Executive Director: Betty Yuan, President Ping Tcheng, Executive Vice-president: Cathy Tsang, Peter Li and other leaders of the group work tirelessly to promote the correct history of the war and particularly try to inform the world of the Japanese atrocities and constantly pressure the Japanese to admit the atrocities, apologize and compensate the enslaved comfort women (sex slaves) and also the enslaved prisoners of the Japanese during the war.

Their research has been extensive and their collection of atrocity pictures are invaluable (many in this book)—a far better collection than in our National Archives (sadly).

Appendices

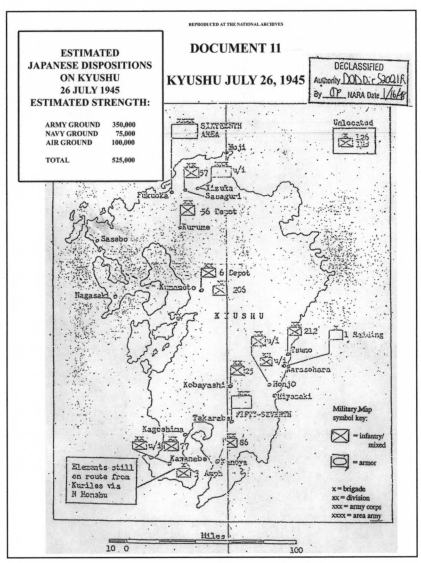

DOCUMENT 11

**ESTIMATED
JAPANESE DISPOSITIONS
ON KYUSHU
26 JULY 1945
ESTIMATED STRENGTH:**

ARMY GROUND	350,000
NAVY GROUND	75,000
AIR GROUND	100,000
TOTAL	525,000

KYUSHU JULY 26, 1945

DECLASSIFIED
Authority DODDir 52001R
By OP NARA Date 1/16/48

Unlocated

Military Map
symbol key:

⊠ = infantry/
mixed

▢ = armor

x = brigade
xx = division
xxx = army corps
xxxx = area army

Elements still
on route from
Kuriles via
N Honshu

Miles
10 0   100

Central Intelligence Agency Monograph

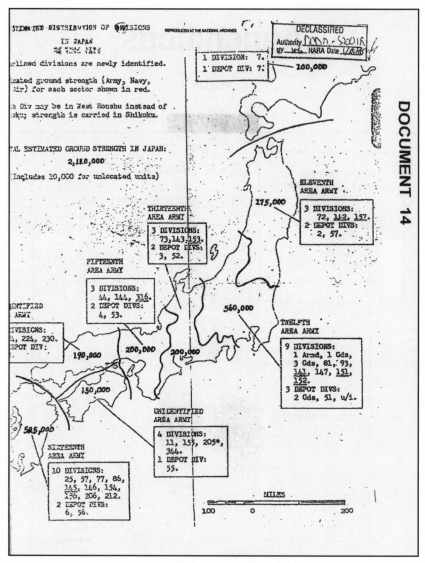

STIMATED DISTRIBUTION OF DIVISIONS
IN JAPAN
AS THAT DATE

...rlined divisions are newly identified.

...mated ground strength (Army, Navy,
...ir) for each sector shown in red.

...h Div may be in West Honshu instead of
...oku; strength is carried in Shikoku.

...AL ESTIMATED GROUND STRENGTH IN JAPAN:
2,110,000
(Includes 10,000 for unlocated units)

REPRODUCED AT THE NATIONAL ARCHIVES

DECLASSIFIED
Authority NND - 52001R
BY NARA Date

1 DIVISION: 7.
1 DEPOT DIV: 7.   100,000

ELEVENTH
AREA ARMY
175,000
3 DIVISIONS:
72, 142, 157.
2 DEPOT DIVS:
2, 57.

THIRTEENTH
AREA ARMY
3 DIVISIONS:
73, 143, 153.
2 DEPOT DIVS:
3, 52.

FIFTEENTH
AREA ARMY
3 DIVISIONS:
44, 144, 216.
2 DEPOT DIVS:
4, 53.

560,000

TWELFTH
AREA ARMY
9 DIVISIONS:
1 Armd, 1 Gds,
3 Gds, 81, 93,
141, 147, 151,
152.
3 DEPOT DIVS:
2 Gds, 51, u/i.

...ENTIFIED
ARMY
...IVISIONS:
..., 224, 230.
...EPOT DIV:

190,000   200,000   200,000

150,000

UNIDENTIFIED
AREA ARMY
4 DIVISIONS:
11, 155, 205*,
344.
1 DEPOT DIV:
55.

585,000

SIXTEENTH
AREA ARMY
10 DIVISIONS:
25, 57, 77, 86,
145, 146, 154,
156, 206, 212.
2 DEPOT DIVS:
6, 56.

MILES
100   0   200

Central Intelligence Agency Monograph

DOCUMENT 14

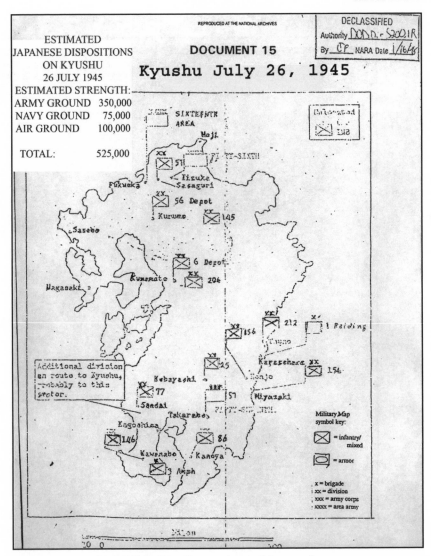

REPRODUCED AT THE NATIONAL ARCHIVES

ESTIMATED
JAPANESE DISPOSITIONS
ON KYUSHU
26 JULY 1945

DOCUMENT 15

Kyushu July 26, 1945

ESTIMATED STRENGTH:
ARMY GROUND   350,000
NAVY GROUND   75,000
AIR GROUND   100,000

TOTAL: 525,000

SIXTEENTH AREA

Moji

Fukuoka

Iizuka
Sasaguri

56 Depot

Kurume

Sasebo

6 Depot

Kumamoto

206

Nagasaki

156

212

1 Raiding

Tsuno

Kagoshima

Kagoshima

146

Kawanabe

Kanoya

3 Amph

Additional division en route to Kyushu, probably to this sector.

Kobayashi

77

Sendai

Takarabe

86

Karasehara

154

Honjo

Miyazaki

57

Military Map
symbol key:

= infantry/
mixed

= armor

x = brigade
xx = division
xxx = army corps
xxxx = area army

Miles

0

Central Intelligence Agency Monograph

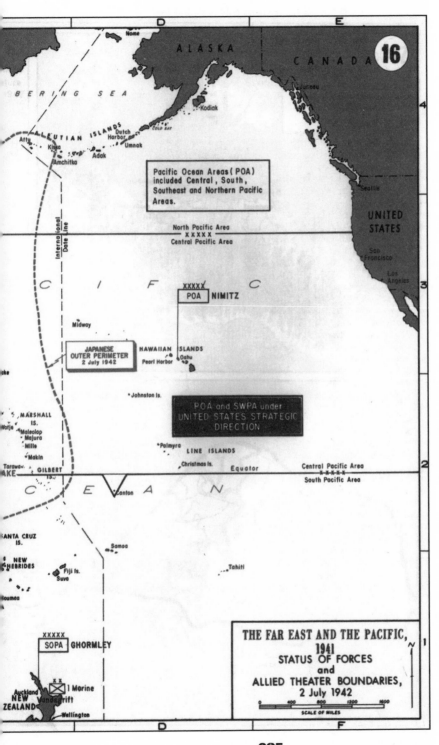

Pacific Ocean Areas (POA)
included Central, South,
Southeast and Northern Pacific
Areas.

North Pacific Area
X X X X X
Central Pacific Area

POA NIMITZ

JAPANESE
OUTER PERIMETER
2 July 1942

POA and SWPA under
UNITED STATES STRATEGIC
DIRECTION

Central Pacific Area
X X X X X
South Pacific Area

SOPA GHORMLEY

1 Marine

THE FAR EAST AND THE PACIFIC,
1941
STATUS OF FORCES
and
ALLIED THEATER BOUNDARIES,
2 July 1942

SCALE OF MILES
0   400   800   1200   1600

Document 62
Papers of Harry S. Truman: President's Secretary's Files

THE WHITE HOUSE
WASHINGTON

January 12, 1953

My dear Professor Cates:

Your letter of December 6, 1952 has just now been delivered to me.

When the message came to Potsdam that a successful atomic explosion had taken place in New Mexico, there was much excitement and conversation about the effect on the war then in progress with Japan.

The next day I told the Prime Minister of Great Britain and Generalissimo Stalin that the explosion had been a success. The British Prime Minister understood and appreciated what I'd told him. Premier Stalin smiled and thanked me for reporting the explosion to him, but I'm sure he did not understand its significance.

I called a meeting of the Secretary of State, Mr. Byrnes, the Secretary of War, Mr. Stimson, Admiral Leahy, General Marshall, General Eisenhower, Admiral King and some others, to discuss what should be done with this awful weapon.

I asked General Marshall what it would cost in lives to land on the Tokio plain and other places in Japan. It was his opinion that such an invasion would cost at a minimum one quarter of a million casualties, and night cost as much as a million, on the American side alone, with an equal number of the enemy. The other military and naval men present agreed.

I asked Secretary Stimson which cities in Japan were devoted exclusively to war production. He promptly named Hiroshima and Nagasaki, among others.

We sent an ultimatum. It was rejected.

I ordered atomic bombs dropped on the two cities named on the way back from Potsdam, when we were in the middle of the Atlanta Ocean.

In your letter, you raise the fact that the directive to General Speats to prepare for delivering the bomb is dated July twenty-fifth. It was, of course, necessary to set the military wheels in motions, as these orders did, but the final decision was in my hands, and was not made until we were returning from Potsdam.

Dropping the bombs ended the war, saved lives, and gave the free nations a chance to face the facts.

When it looked as if Japan would quit, Russia hurried into the fray less than a week before its surrender, so as to be in at the settlement. No military contribution was made by the Russians toward victory over Japan. Prisoners were surrendered and Manchuria occupied by the Soviets, as was Korea, north of the 38th parallel.

Sincerely yours,

(Sgd) HARRY S. TRUMAN

Professor James L. Cate,
Department of History,
The University of Chicago,
1126 East 59th Street,
Chicago 37, Illinois.

THE YALTA AGREEMENT

Between the Leaders of the Three Great Powers—
The United States of America
The Union of Soviet Socialists Republics
and the United Kingdom of Great Britain and
Northern Ireland

Signed at the Yalta February 11, 1945

The leaders of the three Great Powers—the Soviet Union, the United States of America and Great Britain—have agreed that in two or three months after Germany has surrendered and the war in Europe has terminated, the Soviet Union shall enter into the war against Japan on the side of the Allies on condition that:

1. The status quo in Outer-Mongolia (The Mongolian People's Republic) shall be preserved;
2. The former rights of Russia violated by the treacherous attack of Japan in 1904 shall be restored, viz:
    (a) The southern part of Sakhalin as well as all the islands adjacent to it shall be returned to the Soviet Union,
    (b) The commercial port of Dairen shall be internationalized, the preeiminent interests of the Soviet Union in this port being safeguarded and the lease of Port Author as a naval base of the USSR restored.
    (c) The Chinese-Eastern Railroad and the South-Manchurian Railroad which provides an outlet to Dairen shall be jointly operated by the establishment of a joint Soviet-Chinese Company it being understood that the preeiminent interests of the Soviet Union shall be safeguarded and that China shall retain full sovereignty in Manchuria;
3. The Kuril Islands shall be handed over to the Soviet Union.

It is understood, that the agreement concerning Outer-Mongolia and the ports and railroads referred to above will require concurrence of Generalissimo Chiang Kai-Shek. The President will take measures in order to obtain this concurrence on advice from Marshal Stalin.

The Heads of the three Great Powers have agreed that these claims of the Soviet Union shall be unquestionably fulfilled after Japan has been defeated.

For its part the Soviet Union expresses its readiness to conclude with the National Government of China a pact of friendship and alliance between the USSR and China in order to render assistance to China with its armed forced for the purpose of liberating China from the Japanese yoke.

J. Stalin*
Franklin D. Roosevelt
Winston S. Churchill
February 11, 1945

---

* Revised to accord with English usage

THE POTSDAM PROCLAMATION

July 26, 1945

(1) WE—THE PRESIDENT of the United States, the President of the National Government of the Republic of China, and the Prime Minister of Great Britain, representing the hundreds of millions of our countrymen, have conferred and agree that Japan shall be given the opportunity to end this war.

(2) The prodigious land, sea and air forces of the United States, the British Empire and of China, many times reinforced by their armies and air fleets from the west, are poised to strike the final blow upon Japan. This military power is sustained and inspired by the determination of all Allied Nations to prosecute the war against Japan until she ceases to resist.

(3) The result of the futile and senseless German resistance to the might of the aroused free peoples of the world stands forth in awful clarity as an example to the people of Japan. The might that now converges on Japan is immeasurably greater than that which, when applied to the resisting Nazis, necessarily laid waste to the lands, the industry, and the method of life of the whole German people. The full application of our military power, backed by our resolve, *will* mean the inevitable and complete destruction of Japanese armed forces and just as inevitably the utter devastation of the Japanese homeland.

(4) The time has come for Japan to decide whether she will continue to be controlled by those self-willed militaristic advisers whose unintelligent calculations have brought the Empire of Japan to the threshold of annihilation, or whether she will follow the path of reason.

(5) Following are our terms: We will not deviate from them. There are no alternatives. We shall brook no delay.

(6) There must be eliminated from for all time the authority and influence of those who have deceived and misled the people of Japan into embarking in world conquest, for we insist that a new order of peace, security and justice will be impossible until irresponsible militarism is driven from the world.

(7) Until such a new order is established *and* until there is convincing proof that Japan's war-making power is destroyed, points in Japanese territory to be designated by the Allies shall be occupied to secure achievement of the basic objectives we are here setting forth.

(8) The terms of the Cairo Declaration shall be carried out and Japanese sovereignty shall be limited to the islands of Honshu, Hokkaido, Kyushu, Shikoku and such minor islands as we determine.

(9) The Japanese military forces, after being completely disarmed, shall be permitted to return to their homes with the opportunity to lead peaceful and productive lives.

(10) We do not intend that the Japanese shall be enslaved as a race or destroyed as a nation, but stern justice shall be meted out to all war criminals, including those who have visited cruelties upon our prisoners. The Japanese Government shall remove all obstacles to the revival and strengthening of democratic tendencies among the Japanese people. Freedom of speech, of religion, and of thought, as well as respect for the fundamental human rights shall be established.

(11) Japan shall be permitted to maintain such industries as will sustain her economy and permit the exaction of just reparations in kind, but not those which would enable her to re-arm for war. To this end, access to, as distinguished from control of, raw materials shall be permitted. Eventual Japanese participation in world trade relations shall be permitted.

(12) The occupying forces of the Allies shall be withdrawn from Japan as soon as these objectives have been accomplished and there has been established in accordance with the freely expressed will of the Japanese people a peacefully inclined and responsible government.

(13) We call upon the government of Japan to proclaim now the unconditional surrender of all Japanese armed forces, and to provide proper and adequate assurances of their good faith in such action. The alternative for Japan is prompt and utter destruction.

JAPAN'S FIRST SURRENDER OFFER

THE HONORABLE   *August 10, 1945*
JAMES F. BYRNES
Secretary of State

SIR:

I have the honor to inform you that the Japanese Minister to Switzerland, upon instructions received from his Government, has requested the Swiss Political Department to advise the Government of the United States of America of the following:

"In obedience to the gracious command of His Majesty the Emperor who, ever anxious to enhance the cause of world peace, desires earnestly to bring about a speedy termination of hostilities with a view to saving mankind from the calamities to be imposed upon them by further continuation of the war, the Japanese Government several weeks ago asked the Soviet Government, with which neutral relations then prevailed, to render good offices in restoring peace vis a vis the enemy powers. Unfortunately, these efforts in the interest of peace having failed, the Japanese Government in conformity with the august wish of His Majesty to restore the general peace and desiring to put an end to the untold sufferings entailed by war as quickly as possible, have decided upon the following:

"The Japanese Government are ready to accept the terms enumerated in the joint declaration which was issued at Potsdam on July 26th, 1945, by the heads of the Governments of the United States, Great Britain, and China; and later subscribed by the Soviet Government, with the understanding that the said declaration does not comprise any demand which prejudices the prerogatives of His Majesty as a Sovereign Ruler.

"The Japanese Government sincerely hope that this understanding is warranted and desire keenly than an explicit indication to that effect will be speedily forthcoming."

In transmitting the above message the Japanese minister added that his Government begs the Government of the United States to forward its answer through the intermediary of Switzerland. Similar requests are being transmitted to the Governments of Great Britain and the Union of Soviet Socialist Republics through the intermediary of Sweden, as well as to the Government of China through the intermediary of Switzerland. The Chinese Minister at Berne has already been informed of the foregoing through the channel of the Swiss Political Department.

Please be assured that I am at your disposal at any time to accept for and forward to my government the reply of the Government of the United States.

Accept [etc.]

GRASSLI
*Charge d' Affaires ad interim
of Switzerland.*

REPLY TO JAPAN'S FIRST SURRENDER OFFER

By Secretary of State Byrnes

MR. MAX GRASSLI   *August 11, 1945*
Charge d' Affaires ad interim
of Switzerland

SIR:
    I have the honor to acknowledge the receipt of your note of
August 10, and in reply to inform you that the President of United
States has directed me to send to you for transmission by Government
to the Japanese Government the following message on behalf of the
Governments of the United States, the United Kingdom, the Union of
Soviet Socialist Republics, and China;
    "With regard to the Japanese Government's message accepting the
terms of the Potsdam proclamation but containing the statement,
'with the understanding that the said declaration does not comprise
any demand which prejudices the prerogatives of His Majesty as a
sovereign ruler, our position is as follows:
    "The Emperor will be required to authorize and ensure the
signature by the Government of Japan and the Japanese Imperial
General Headquarters of the surrender terms necessary to carry
out the provisions of the Potsdam Declaration, and shall issue his
commands to all the Japanese military, naval and air authorities
and to all the forces under their control wherever located to cease
active operations and to surrender their arms, and to issue such
other orders as the Supreme Commander may require to give effect to
the surrender terms.
    "Immediately upon the surrender the Japanese Government shall
transport prisoners of war and civilian internees to places of
safety, as directed, where they can quickly be placed aboard Allied
transports.
    "The ultimate form of government of Japan shall, in accordance
with the Potsdam Declaration, be established by the freely expressed
will of the Japanese people.
    "The armed forces of the Allied Powers will remain in Japan until
the purposes set forth in the Potsdam Declaration are achieved."

Accept [etc.]

                            JAMES F. BYRNES
                            Secretary of State

THE IMPERIAL RESCRIPT OF AUGUST 14, 1945

TO OUR GOOD AND LOYAL SUBJECTS:

After pondering deeply the general trends of the world and the actual conditions obtaining in Our Empire today, We have decided to effect a settlement of the present situation by resorting to an extraordinary measure.

We have ordered Our Government to communicate to the Governments of the United States, Great Britain, China, and the Soviet Union that Our Empire accepts the provisions of their Joint Declaration.

To strive for the common prosperity and happiness of all nations as well as the security and well-being of Our subjects is the solemn obligation which has been handed down by Our Imperial Ancestors, and which We lay close to heart. Indeed, We declared war on America and Britain out of Our sincere desire to ensure Japan's self preservation and the stabilization of East Asia, it being far from Our thought either to infringe upon the sovereignty of other nations or to embark upon territorial aggrandizement. But now the war has lasted for nearly four years. Despite the best that has been done by everyone—the gallant fighting of military and naval forces, the diligence and assiduity of Our servants of the State and the devoted service of Our one hundred million people, the war situation has developed not necessarily to Japan's advantage, while the general trends of the world have all turned against her interest. Moreover, the enemy has begun to employ a new and most cruel bomb, the power of which to do damage is indeed incalculable, taking the roll of many innocent lives. Should We continue to fight, it would not only result in an ultimate collapse and obliteration of the Japanese nation, but also it would lead to the total extinction of human civilization. Such being the case, are We to save the millions of Our subjects; or to atone Ourselves before the hallowed spirits of Our Imperial Ancestors? This is the reason why We have ordered the acceptance of the provisions of the Joint Declaration of the Powers.

We cannot express the deepest sense of regret to our Allied nations of East Asia, who have consistently cooperated with the Empire towards the emancipation of East Asia. The thought of those officers and men as well as others who have fallen in the fields of battle, those who died at their posts of duty, or those who met with untimely death and all their bereaved families, pains Our heart night and day. The welfare of the wounded and the war-sufferers, and of those who have lost their homes and livelihood, are the objects of Our profound solicitude. The hardships and sufferings to which Our nation is to be subjected hereafter will certainly be great. We are keenly aware of the inmost feelings of all ye, Our subjects. However it is according to the dictate of time and fate that We have resolved to pave the way for a grand peace for all the generations to come by enduring the unendurable and suffering what is insufferable.

Having been able to safeguard and maintain the structure of the Imperial State, We are always with ye, Our good and loyal subjects, relying upon your sincerity and integrity. Beware most strictly of any outbursts of emotion, which may engender needless complications, or any fraternal contention and strife which may create confusion, lead ye astray and cause ye to lose the confidence in the world. Let the entire nation continue as one family from generation to generation, ever firm in its faith of the imperishableness of its divine land, and mindful of its heavy burden of responsibilities, and the long road before it. Unite your total strength to be devoted to the construction for the future. Cultivate the ways of rectitude; foster nobility of spirit; and work with resolution so as ye may enhance the innate glory of the Imperial State and keep peace with the progress of the world.

(Imperial Sign Manual)
(Imperial Seal)

The 14th day pf the 8th month
Of the 20th year of Showa.

INSTRUMENT OF SURRENDER

September 2, 1945 (Tokyo Time)

We, acting by command of any in behalf of the Emperor of Japan, the Japanese Government and the Japanese Imperial General Headquarters, hereby accept the provisions set forth in the declaration issued by the heads of the Governments of the United States, China and Great Britain on 26 July 1945, at Potsdam, and subsequently adhered to by the Union of the Soviet Socialist Republics, which four powers are hereafter referred to as the Allied Powers.

We hereby proclaim the unconditional surrender to the Allied Powers of the Japanese Imperial General Headquarters of all Japanese armed forces and all armed forced under Japanese control wherever situated.

We hereby command all Japanese forces wherever situated and the Japanese people to cease hostilities forthwith, to preserve and save from damage all ships, aircraft, and military and civil property and to comply with all requirements which may be imposed by the Supreme Commander for the Allied Powers or by agencies of the Japanese Government at his direction.

We hereby command the Japanese Imperial General Headquarters to issue at once orders to the Commander of all Japanese forces and all forces under Japanese control wherever situated to surrender unconditionally themselves and all forced under their control.

We hereby command all civil, military and naval officials to obey and enforce all proclamations, orders and directives deemed by the Supreme Commander for the Allied Powers to be proper to effectuate this surrender and issued by him or under his authority and we direct all such officials to remain at their posts and to continue to perform their non-combatant duties unless specifically relieved by him or under his authority.

We hereby undertake for the Emperor, the Japanese Government and their successors to carry out the provisions of the Potsdam Declaration in good faith, and to issue whatever orders and take whatever action may be required by the Supreme Commander for the Allied Powers or by any other designated representative of the Allied Powers for the purpose of giving effect to that Declaration.

We hereby command the Japanese Imperial Government and the Japanese Imperial General Headquarters at once to liberate all allied prisoners of war and civilian internees now under Japanese control and to provide for their protection, care, maintenance and immediate transportation to places as directed.

The authority of the Emperor and the Japanese Government to rule the state shall be subject to the Supreme Commander for the Allied Powers who will take such steps as he deems proper to effectuate those terms of surrender.

Signed at *Toyko Bay, Japan* at *0904 I* on the *second* day of *September*, 1945.

> MAMORU SHIGEMITSU*
>> By Command and in behalf of the Emperor of Japan
>> And the Japanese Government.

> YOSHIJIRO UMEZU*
>> By Command and in behalf of the Japanese
>> Imperial General Headquarters

Accepted at *Tokyo Bay, Japan*, at *0908 I* on the *second* day of *September*, 1945.
for the United States, Republic of China, United Kingdom and the Union of Soviet Socialist Republics, and in the interests of the other United Nations at war with Japan.

> DOUGLAS MACARTHUR
>> *Supreme Commander for the Allied Powers.* †

---

* Romanized to accord with English usage.
† General MacArthur's signature is followed by those of C.W. Nimitz (United States Representative), Yung-ch'ang Hsü* (Republic of China), Bruce Fraser (United Kingdom), General-Lietenant K. Derevyanko (Union of Soviet Socialist Republics), T.A. Blamey (Commonwealth of Australia) , L. Moore Cosgrave (Dominion of Canada), Leclerc (Provisional Government of the French Republic) C.E.L. Helfrich (Kingdom of the Netherlands), Leonard M. Isitt (Dominion of New Zealand).

THE IMPERIAL RESCRIPT OF SEPTEMBER 2, 1945

Accepting the terms set forth in Declaration issued by the heads of the Governments of the United States, Great Britain and China on July 26th, 1945 at Potsdam and subsequently adhered to by the Union of Soviet Socialist Republics, We have commanded the Japanese Imperial Government and the Japanese Imperial General Headquarters to sign on Our behalf the Instrument of Surrender presented by the Supreme Commander for the Allied Powers and to issue General Orders to the Military and Naval Forces in accordance with the direction of the Supreme Commander for the Allied Powers. We command all Our people forthwith to cease hostilities, to lay down their arms and faithfully carry out all the provisions of Instrument of Surrender and the General Orders issued by the Japanese Imperial Government and the Japanese Imperial general Headquarters hereunder.

This second day of the ninth month of the twentieth year of Syowa.

Seal of
   the   HIROHITO
Emperor

NARUHIKO-O
  Prime Minister

MAMORU SHIGEMITSU
  Minister of Foreign Affairs

IWAO YAMAZAKI
  Minister of Finance

JUICHI TSUSHIMA
  Minister of Finance

SADAMU SHIMOMURA
  Minister of War

MITSUMASA YONAI
  Minister of Navy

CHUZO IWATA
  Minister of Justice

TAMON MAEDA
  Minister of Education

KENZO MATSUMURA
  Minister of Welfare

KOTARO SENGOKU
  Minister of Agriculture and Forestry

CHIKUHEI NAKAJIMA
  Minister of Commerce

NAOTO KOBIYAMA
  Minister of Transportation

FUMIMARO KONOE
  Minister without Portfolio

TAKETORA OGATA
  Minister without Portfolio

BINSHIRO OBATA
  Minister without Portfolio

In Gratitude

Many people need to be thanked for helping with this book.

Beth Newman and Mary Henry, Legal Assistants in the law office of my sons, Frank C. Winn and Nick Winn. In their spare time at the office they completed the monumental task of typing and helping me edit this book.

Frank C. Winn and Nick Winn, for letting me use their office and work with Beth and Mary on the book.

Darice W. Lewis (my daughter) for helping me organize the entire book.

My good friend **Doug Elliott,** who very diligently searched the internet for material I needed at the beginning of this project.

Brenda Dempsey, in her spare time, did a great job typing (and retyping) all of my original edition of Clear Conscience.

Dick Campbell, of Albuquerque, NM, helped obtain pictures of the mushroom cloud, courtesy of the National Atomic Museum.

Senator Sam Nunn was very helpful.

Carol Leadenham of the Hoover Institution, Stanford University was very gracious in guiding me through some research at the Institute.

Raul Goco, the Solicitor General of the Philippines, and a great friend, provided me with the great chapter "Rape of Manila."

Karen Parker, an expert on the "Comfort Women," provided me with some excellent material.

Alex Albert in Senator Paul Coverdell's office helped me get in touch with General Tibbets at the beginning of the project.

Johnson Printing Company, in Cedartown, GA, a big help.

Bob Steed, my good friend and author, was most helpful.

Dick Parker, a Cedartown friend and publisher of "Looking Glass Books," has been a great help.

Alex Hawkins, this good friend, ex-NFL player, and great humorous author gave me much encouragement.

Kiela's Photo Lab, Cedartown, Georgia (Kiela Beam, owner) has done a superb job on the pictures, maps and cover for the book.

Members of the **"Alliance for Preserving the Truth of the Sino-Japanese War"** have worked with me during the entire book project. **Ignatius Ding** has worked with me constantly. **Betty Yuan, President,** has given me tremendous support. **Kansen Chu**, the former Chairperson of the Alliance, and his wife, **Daisy Chu,** along with **Eugene L. Wei, Victor Yung, Tony Chang** (*Sing Tao Daily*), **Cathy Tsang** (a founding vice president of the Alliance) and other members of the Alliance, honored me with a great informative luncheon (true history lesson) at the Ocean Harbor Restaurant, San Jose, CA. Kansen and Daisy, owners of the restaurant, provided one of the best gourmet meals I have ever enjoyed. Ping and Jane Tcheng have helped me on this latest edition; Professor Gregory Tsang has also been helpful on this edition.

Many thanks go to **Brigadier General Paul W. Tibbets, Jr.** for our many discussions concerning the use of the Bomb and the revisionists and how to answer them. Everyone should read his revised book, *Flight of the Enola Gay*. General Tibbets passed away at age 92 on Thursday Nov. 1, 2007.

Deepest thanks go to **General Ray Davis** for joining me in this book and aiding greatly in its credibility. General Davis passed away before this expanded edition could be completed. I consider him one of the greatest military heroes ever and one of the finest men I've ever known.

When I was asked by a friend about the writing of this book I told him, "With a Four Star General and one lowly Marine Major involved, who did you think was going to do the work?"

Judge Dan Winn (Scrivener)
Senior Judge
Superior Courts of Georgia

Served with the U.S. Marine Air Corps in WWII in the Pacific. Distinguished Flying Cross and Air Medals.

Index